Pra
*Loving Your Black*

"In this wonderful work, Chanté ...helps us develop a trans-formational vision of anti-racism and consistently equips the reader to take concrete steps in living this out. But what made this book most unique for me was the way she takes us into the deepest of all mysteries: the ability to love. She shows us that, at its core, love is a multidimensional reality and that any ability we develop to live an anti-racist kind of life will always find itself built on the foundation of multidimensional love."

—DANIEL HILL, pastor and author of *White Awake* and *White Lies*

"Chanté Griffin beautifully defines *and* refines what it means to love your Black Neighbor at every turn in this book. And she does so by offering an essential combination of research, mindfulness, and stories of her own lived experience and observations—all while being unapologetically Black on the page.

Without being didactic, Chanté outlines intentional ways white readers of faith can move beyond black boxes on social media and conspiratorial whispers of solidarity, and toward distinct, compassionate actions that provide safety and accountability. *Loving Your Black Neighbor as Yourself* truly eliminates any and all excuses for the race-related chasm that exists between white and Black believers. Readers will inevitably end each chapter with 'Selah' as Chanté offers Christ-centered lenses to those who are willing to wear them and see their Black brothers and sisters anew."

—TRACEY MICHAE'L LEWIS-GIGGETTS,
author of *Then They Came for Mine: Healing
from the Trauma of Racial Violence*
and the forthcoming *Black Joy Playbook*

"*Loving Your Black Neighbor as Yourself* is a beautifully written book that calls forth deep meditation on both spirit and practice. Chanté Griffin demonstrates clearly that love and justice are strands of one thread in the work of racial wholeness. She shows white Christians who love Jesus how to manifest that relationship in the daily ways we live as we walk with, beside, and for Black people and their sacred flourishing. There is no abstraction here. The material conditions of our daily ways of being are called into account in this profoundly wise book."

—Dr. Jennifer Harvey,
author of *Antiracism as Daily Practice* and *Raising White Kids*

"*Loving Your Black Neighbor as Yourself* is more than just a book; it's a movement toward a more loving, understanding, and inclusive society. At its core, this guide is about closing the space between individuals and their Black Neighbors. Griffin masterfully navigates the complexities of these relationships, offering insights that are both profound and accessible. Whether you're seeking to deepen your understanding, build stronger community bonds, or simply be a part of positive change, this book is a must-read. Griffin's guide is a heartfelt invitation to embark on a journey of love, learning, and lasting transformation. It's a call to action, a road map to a better world, and a testament to the power of love to bridge the deepest of divides. Read it, live it, and be a part of the change we all wish to see in the world."

—Dr. Elizabeth Rios,
founder of Passion2Plant church planting network

"Griffin expertly guides us through research, personal narrative, and Scripture with a writer's skill, prophetic insight, and above all, the spirit of love. This book offers practical and personal ways to love our Black Neighbors as ourselves, all the while caring for readers with pauses for reflection and check-ins. Love isn't just the subject of this book; it's woven throughout every page and paragraph to create a tapestry of the beauty, flourishing, and joy that comes from loving our Black Neighbors as ourselves."

—DR. AMY KENNY, author of *My Body Is Not a Prayer Request*

"For fellow white Christians like myself who desire to broaden our understanding of the African American experience in the United States, this book is an invaluable resource. With its capacity to foster greater empathy, awareness, and compassion, it equips us to extend love and understanding to Christians navigating a world that may differ from our own. Griffin's work invites us to embark on a transformative journey toward a more inclusive and loving Christian community."

—J. W. BUCK, PhD, author of *Everyday Activism*

"*Loving Your Black Neighbor as Yourself* is a glory and a gift. This exciting writer dares to make us laugh, cry, and fall on our amazed faces with enough glee and grace to grow in actual love. An instant classic, Griffin's plea is thrumming with wise hope—lighting the way to knowing and loving Black Neighbors so bravely that we know and love God and ourselves even more. A practical and powerful journey; it's worth every uplifting and honest step."

—PATRICIA RAYBON, author of *My First White Friend*

# LOVING

## YOUR BLACK NEIGHBOR AS YOURSELF

# LOVING
## YOUR BLACK NEIGHBOR
## AS YOURSELF

*A Guide to Closing the Space Between Us*

# CHANTÉ GRIFFIN

WATERBROOK

All Scripture quotations, unless otherwise indicated, are taken from the Holy Bible, New International Version®, NIV®. Copyright © 1973, 1978, 1984, 2011 by Biblica Inc.™ Used by permission of Zondervan. All rights reserved worldwide. (www.zondervan.com). The "NIV" and "New International Version" are trademarks registered in the United States Patent and Trademark Office by Biblica Inc.™ Scripture quotations marked (CSB) are taken from the Christian Standard Bible®, copyright © 2017 by Holman Bible Publishers. Used by permission. Christian Standard Bible® and CSB® are federally registered trademarks of Holman Bible Publishers. Scripture quotations marked (KJV) are taken from the King James Version. Scripture quotations marked (NKJV) are taken from the New King James Version®. Copyright © 1982 by Thomas Nelson. Used by permission. All rights reserved. Scripture quotations marked (NLT) are taken from the Holy Bible, New Living Translation, copyright © 1996, 2004, 2015 by Tyndale House Foundation. Used by permission of Tyndale House Publishers, Carol Stream, Illinois 60188. All rights reserved.

Italics in Scripture quotations reflect the author's added emphasis.

A WaterBrook Trade Paperback Original

Published in the United States by WaterBrook, an imprint of Random House, a division of Penguin Random House LLC.

WATERBROOK and colophon are registered trademarks of Penguin Random House LLC.

Library of Congress Cataloging-in-Publication Data
Names: Griffin, Chanté, author.
Title: Loving your Black neighbor as yourself: a guide to closing the space between us / Chanté Griffin.
Description: Colorado Springs: WaterBrook, [2024] | Includes bibliographical references.
Identifiers: LCCN 2023039945 | ISBN 9780593445594 (trade paperback; acid-free paper) | ISBN 9780593445600 (ebook)
Subjects: LCSH: Race relations—Religious aspects—Christianity. | Reconciliation—Religious aspects—Christianity. | African Americans—Race relations. | Golden rule.
Classification: LCC BT734.2 .G73 2024 | DDC 261/.108996073—dc23/eng/20231221
LC record available at https://lccn.loc.gov/2023039945

Printed in the United States of America on acid-free paper

waterbrookmultnomah.com

9 8 7 6 5 4 3 2 1

*Book design by Diane Hobbing*

Most WaterBrook books are available at special quantity discounts for bulk purchase for premiums, fundraising, and corporate and educational needs by organizations, churches, and businesses. Special books or book excerpts also can be created to fit specific needs. For details, contact specialmarketscms@penguinrandomhouse.com.

*To my mother, Vivi, who taught me to love God with all my heart, soul, mind, and strength; to my father, Bobby, who taught me to pursue my dreams; and to Aunt Jackie, my godmother, who remained resolute in God's goodness until the end.*

# CONTENTS

## Part Three: Go and Do Likewise

# BEFORE YOU BEGIN

Blackness is my mother tongue, my very first love language.

I was birthed in a Black Pentecostal church. My dark-skinned body was birthed into choir rocks and hand claps, my spirit reborn in the cool baptismal pool. My speech refined with new tongues, and my future prophesied into being.

I don't remember my parents (barely adults themselves) keeping my little sister and me on any precious sleeping schedule: *6:00 dinner, 7:00 bath, 8:00 bedtime story.* I do remember falling asleep at church to the sound of the drummer's snare and the organ's sirens. I remember women shouting and wailing and being ensconced by other women in white who fanned them as they lay outstretched on the floor, discreetly covered by white sheets.

My sis and me were "church babies"—children whose sleep can withstand the preacher's whoops and the congregation's hollers, permanent fixtures at most Black Pentecostal churches. We usually passed out on the pews, clutching our children's Bibles to keep Satan from prying them from us. Sometimes we wore bows in our hair and lace on our socks, accented by the black patent leather shoes our mothers bought us for Easter service. Sometimes we sported little wool jackets and bow ties that matched our fathers'. We'd been taught we must *always* look good for God.

I remember children's church, where I learned that "Jesus loves the little children, all the children of the world: Red and yellow, black and white, they are precious in His sight."[1] I remember Sunday night service, Thursday night Bible study, and Saturday morning choir rehearsal.

For the first ten years of my life, my world was completely Black. I attended an all-Black church in South Central Los Angeles and that church's all-Black private Christian school, and my family lived in an adjacent all-Black neighborhood. I remember only one exception to this all-Black world: Cindy, the only non-Black person in our entire K–8 school. Cindy was Filipina, wore a short bob with bangs, and always had a lot of money. And when I say "a lot of money," I mean five dollars.

I knew about other racial groups, but I never interacted with them. My experience was not uncommon for a young Black girl living in South Central Los Angeles in the 1980s.

The Black world was the only one I knew. And it felt safe, even with the helicopters that sometimes flew above my neighborhood as I played double Dutch with my friends on the cracked concrete pavement. To us, Blackness was as natural and unassuming as the daily sunrise. It's amazing how much self-esteem we built as the standard and not the deviant.

I didn't know to cherish these moments. I didn't know that my world would turn upside down when my parents decided we were "movin' on up"[2] to a neighborhood in the San Fernando Valley, where my sister and I would become two of four Black kids in an entire elementary school. There, I learned that the outside world didn't just not see us. It didn't love us.

## From My Heart to the Page

When my family left our all-Black world in South L.A. in 1988, I became aware of racism for the first time. That's when I first saw the robbery: Most of the Black students weren't tracked into the honors and advanced-placement classes in school, despite their undeniable brilliance. Resources for schools, parks, and jobs often bypassed areas with large Black populations and went straight to more affluent, predominantly white neighborhoods. My neighbors tried to rob me of my dignity by calling me the N-word, insisting my Black skin wasn't beautiful, and purposefully looking past me to serve the white man behind me in line.

Inside my all-Black world, all I felt was love, but outside it, I could see the loveless forces that had crammed us together in a "concrete jungle" in hope of never having to be neighbors with us. In my new multiracial world, love was as consistent as fleeting middle school crushes, and the inconsistency would mark my psyche for years to come.

They say that your childhood experiences lay the foundation for your future. They're right.

I've spent most of my career intentionally serving my Black Neighbors. First as a university chaplain working with Black collegians and then as a director at a non-profit primarily serving Black and Latino/a students. Today as a journalist, I write about the intersection of race, culture, and faith. Like actor Cuba Gooding, Jr., declared in the film *Jerry Maguire,* "I love Black people!"[3] My love for us is as deep as forever and as wide as eternity. So *Loving Your Black Neighbor as Yourself* is a natural outpouring of my love for Black people—a way to show my love and a guide for others to lavishly love their Black Neighbors.

Partly a "how to" book and partly a "grow into" book, at its core, this is a spiritual formation book designed to help you become someone who loves your Black Neighbor multidimensionally. The first part of the book is designed to help grow your love for God, your Black Neighbor, and yourself. The second part is designed to show you practical ways to love your Black Neighbor.

With this in mind, the book is meant to be experienced rather than simply read. You will encounter prose, poetic interludes, heart checks, imagined reading exercises, and prayer pauses—all designed to help you deeply engage with the material. I encourage you to take your time with every part of this book. When I ask you to pause, please don't skip ahead. Please use every instance as an opportunity to grow. Immerse yourself in the imagination exercises. Honestly search your heart, write your thoughts, and reflect during the checks. Pray, Beloved. Pray like your heart depends on it, because it does. Urgently seek out and engage the Spirit of Love, and the Spirit will engage you right back.* So take your time. Sip the words in this book like a fine wine.

If you're able, read this book alongside community—your family, friends, neighbors, or small group. If you want, host a group discussion or book club meeting. Having others to talk and share with will only help your journey.

Although this book is written primarily to white people and non-Black people of color, it is a love tome meant to love and honor the Black community. This book is for *anyone* who wants to love their Black Neighbor anew. If you're not Black, then this book is definitely for you. If you're Black, then this book may be for you, too, because we aren't necessarily immune from the ways racism, colorism, and classism have colored how we view and love one another. So while some parts of the book may resonate with you more than other parts, I hope the stories in its pages make you feel seen, loved, and honored.

No matter who you are or where you're from, I hope you feel

---

* One of my favorite passages says, "Ask and it will be given to you; seek and you will find; knock and the door will be opened to you" (Matthew 7:7).

seen, loved, and honored as you read. I hope you can receive this book the same way I received it: with an open mind and an open heart.

## Lexicon and Language

Language is critical. It can include, exclude, uplift, and reshape. As we enter this author-reader conversation, a shared language will help connect us. So allow me a moment to get us both on the same page.

### Who Is "Black"?

I write this book from my perspective as an African American woman. In this book, *Black* generally refers to either African Americans or experiences common to African Americans living in the United States. When I use the word *Black,* I seek to capture *some* of the common experiences of being an African American in the U.S. Additionally, I use *Black* as an umbrella term that can encompass experiences of other Black folk living in the States, including recent immigrants from Africa and the Caribbean, for example, who may closely identify with their country of origin. I'm cognizant that their experiences can differ from and mirror the experiences of those who identify as African Americans.

*Black* is capitalized throughout this book to signify honor and respect and because in 2020 *The Associated Press Stylebook* (a style and grammar guidebook used by journalists and other writers) declared that the word should be capitalized when denoting a shared culture and history. But just as importantly, as my writing colleague Janelle Harris Dixon asserted in a 2016 Twitter post, "I always capitalize Black. My editors can change it if they must, but it never leaves me with a lowercase B. We are an uppercase people."[4]

## Your Black Neighbor

Your Black Neighbor is any Black person you come across at any moment in time. Your Black Neighbor is also the collective Black community. Your Black Neighbor can be a colleague at work, a group of Black teenagers playing b-ball at a public park on a warm evening in August, a group of Black parents at your parent-teacher association meeting, or someone you've known since you shared Fruit Roll-Ups in kindergarten.

## Names for God

I've read that there are more than one hundred names for God in the Bible and that in Judaism, the four-letter name of God, YHWH, is forbidden to be uttered because it is considered too holy. Instead, God is often referenced as "Hashem."[5]

I admire how Judaism puts respect on God's name, and I try to do the same throughout this book but differently. I always capitalize references to God to show respect. I also capitalize the name of anyone I want to lavish extra honor on.

Generally, I refer to God as "God," and because I love nicknames, I also refer to God as "the Spirit of Love" or "Love."[6] Theologically, though, I recognize the differences among the Trinity: God the Father, God the Son (Jesus), and God the Holy Spirit.

Last, although God is a spirit and is neither male nor female, I reference God as Scripture does, using male pronouns for God the Father and Jesus the Son.

## African American English

African American English (AAE) is a language that Black folk in the U.S. have spoken for centuries. Occasionally I use AAE as I write, so if you come across a word or phrase or sentence construction that feels odd, then I'm most likely using AAE, and I invite you to either read the footnote I supply or look up the term online. If you don't recognize AAE in this manuscript, then that's a sign of the impact AAE has had on Standard American English.

## Definition of Racism

You'd think it would be easy to define *racism,* but it is anything but easy. There are differing definitions, and racism can take many forms. At the crux of racism are racial hierarchy and the belief that some groups are superior to others and thus are more deserving of certain things. Historian and author of *How to Be an Antiracist* Dr. Ibram X. Kendi defined a racist as "one who is supporting a racist policy through their actions or inaction or expressing a racist idea."[7] Furthering his idea, I define *racism* as "failing to love someone largely—or at least in part—because of their race." I include unconscious bias, racial prejudice, microaggressions, and the sin of partiality to a racial group under the racism label because their impact is the same. When unchecked, racism, in any form, always produces pain and death—in us and our neighbors. I use *racism* as an umbrella term because it speaks to the weight and impact of not loving our Black Neighbors.

Racism can be intentionally or unintentionally espoused by individuals, groups, organizations, corporations, and policies. While white people and people of color can perpetuate racism, I believe the Spirit of Love can replace this *ism* with love.

Throughout the book, I seek to honor God, you the reader, and your Black Neighbor. If you feel like I've somehow missed the mark in how I use language, I apologize and invite you to extend grace and love to me.

## As You Begin the Journey

My hope is that you will engage with this book the way I learned to. Here's what I mean.

When I started to write this book, I thought of it as work to be done. Yes, work I felt called and inspired to do, but work nonetheless. As a result, each weekday at 7:30 A.M., I rushed to grab the corner table at my local Starbucks to write. As the months wore on, I realized that while I initially thought it was my responsibility to work on the book, the book ended up working on me. It required me to face parts of myself I didn't want to see. It demanded that I share from a place of vulnerability and authenticity, in ways I didn't want to. It asked for more of me: more prayer, more research, more love, more compassion. Ultimately, the book grew me into more than I was prior to writing it.

This is my prayer for you: That as you do the work of reading this book, you will allow it to work on you. That you will allow it to show you parts of yourself you haven't wanted to see. That you will allow it to unearth vulnerability and authenticity within you. That you will allow it to ask you for more and grow you into more. I pray that as you become more, your love for your Black Neighbor will become as deep and boundless as the Spirit of Love's love for you.

# PART ONE

# Love

# Love Is . . .

Love is . . .

the wrapping of oneself around another. it's handling someone with gloves to ensure they are well taken care of.

love is gentle and soft like a newborn's tummy. love knows that the other is fragile, that it must handle with care. it makes concessions for the other, which makes love subject, even submissive, to the other. love doesn't mind, though.

love doesn't try to control. love releases the other, releases the other with no expectation. love is the ultimate angel investor: it invests with no expectation of ownership.

love is the needed space and the grace we give to another when they push us away.

love covers another when their nakedness is exposed. love brings figs and blankets and builds a warm fire.

love never fails.

# CHAPTER 1

# Love Yourself

Create in me a clean heart, O God.
Renew a loyal spirit within me.

—Psalm 51:10, NLT

I ran into walls as a toddler. And into sliding glass doors. Turns out I needed glasses, like my father, his mother, and her siblings. And not the cute, stylish kind you can buy from a hip brand like Warby Parker. Imagine a two-year-old with a small body, a big head, and lenses so thick her eyes doubled in size!

True to my four-eyed persona, I was kind of a nerd in school. I *loved* to get good grades on tests, assignments, and pop quizzes—plus, I was doing *all* the extra credit because the only thing better than an A is an A+. Case in point: When I was around ten or eleven, I was determined to ace the eye exam at the optometrist's office, even though I have astigmatism, and let's not forget—I used to run into walls. When I arrived at the eye doctor's office that afternoon for my annual exam, I started to memorize the eye chart: "D, C, T, P . . ."

"What are you doing?" my mom asked as she caught me reciting the letters. My mouth remained silent, but my face clearly communicated that she had caught me.

"Don't do that," she warned. "The doctor needs to know what you can and can't see so he can give you the right lenses to see clearly."

When dealing with difficult racial issues—be it racism, unconscious bias, the sin of partiality, racial prejudice, microaggressions, or anything else—*everybody* wants to ace their eye exam. *No, I didn't say anything racist!* you declare. *No, I didn't do that racist thing!* you insist. *And no, I'm definitely not racist!* you protest. It's easy to hold shame for not seeing your Black Neighbor clearly. It's also easy to avoid admitting there's a deficiency or to cover up the deficiencies in your vision by reciting "D, C, T, P . . ."

But when someone calls you out for saying or doing something racist, you can choose how to respond: Do you allow fear, pride, and shame to wrap themselves around you like a protective blanket, refusing to confess, furthering the pain you've caused? Or do you love yourself, trample shame under your feet, and eagerly undergo an eye exam so you can receive new lenses?

## Love Yourself Fully

When we were children, our parents or guardians regularly took us to the doctor and dentist to make sure our bodies were functioning well. They did this because they loved us and they knew we wouldn't go on our own. Think about it—how many eight-year-olds are like, "Mom, you know what I want for my birthday? A trip to the dentist!"

But today as adults, we take ourselves to the doctor, the dentist, the optometrist, the cardiologist, and more. We take ourselves to appointments because we want to be well. We also recognize that when we aren't well, it affects us *and* everyone around us. For instance, if we don't realize that we need new lenses to see clearly, we will go around running into walls and people. If we stay in denial about the fact that we need lenses, we will continue running into things, hurting ourselves and others. Loving ourselves doesn't stop at doctor visits, though.

In contemporary American culture, we commonly define loving yourself as taking good care of your physical and emotional health by eating well, exercising, carving out "me time," visiting a therapist, and maybe retreating to the spa with your friends or to the man cave with your buddies. Yes, loving yourself can include all of this, but loving yourself also means tending to your spiritual and relational health just as you would your physical and emotional health. Loving yourself requires a multidimensional, holistic love.

The concept of multidimensional love isn't new. In Deuteronomy 6, when God's commandments were given to the Israelites, he said to love him multidimensionally, "with all your heart and with all your soul and with all your strength."[1] In fact, loving God multidimensionally is so important that Jesus called it out again.

In Luke, a religion expert attempted to test Jesus on the law, asking Jesus what he must do to live with God forever. Jesus agreed with the expert's answer to the question, including the addition of loving one's neighbors: "'Love the Lord your God with all your heart and with all your soul and with all your strength and with all your mind'; and, 'Love your neighbor as yourself.'"[2]

God's love for us, and our love for God, is the foundation from which we love ourselves and our neighbors. Loving ourselves multidimensionally, in partnership with the Spirit of Love, is one of the truest ways we love ourselves.

If you love yourself, then you are willing to look at the parts of yourself that need a doctor's tender, loving care. You are willing to receive the wellness package the Spirit of Love has for you, which includes being honest with yourself, God, and your Black Neighbor about the full condition of your heart.

Hearts have eyes—if not literally, then definitely metaphorically, according to Paul Baloche, who penned the popular worship song "Open the Eyes of My Heart."[3] Our hearts hold our innermost beliefs, and they reveal how we see and resultantly treat our Black Neighbors. If we allow our hearts to be examined, they reveal how much (or little) love we have for those neighbors and the ways our love needs to be purified. Our hearts house our fears, our insecurities, our pride, and the parts of us we don't wanna acknowledge. In fact, we don't always know what's in our hearts until someone shows us the results of our eye exam.

Beloved, love yourself by being honest about any ways you haven't viewed your Black Neighbor properly. Allow yourself to be wrapped in God's forgiveness and love. When you seize the opportunity to confront the sin of racism as an opportunity to love yourself, then despite how horrible getting called out may feel, you will embrace it as a gift from God. A gift that can close the space between you, God, and your Black Neighbor.

## Prayer Pause

Confronting any racism in your heart is no easy task. You may think, *Chanté, I don't need to do this—I'm fine!* Or your physical heart may be racing a little because you're afraid of what you may see. Either way, I encourage you to be open to what the Spirit of Love may show you. Whatever it is, it will be good for you *and* your Black Neighbor.

Before we move forward, let's pray for guidance and support from the Spirit of Love. First notice the posture of your body: Are you tense? Holding your breath?

Take a deep breath, in and out, allowing any tension

to leave your body. Then pray this breath prayer. (Breath prayers promote calm and can help your physical body connect with your spirit. As you inhale and exhale, pray the words silently.)

Breathe in:
*Spirit of Love, talking about racism is hard.*

Breathe out:
*Remove any fear or shame I may have.*

Breathe in:
*Give me courage for an eye exam.*

Breathe out:
*Give me grace to love myself anew.*

## Love Yourself: Recognize That Your Heart Could House Racism

In 1906, a Black preacher named William J. Seymour led the Azusa Street Revival in California. Blacks, whites, and their Chinese, Mexican, and other neighbors worshipped God together freely during the event.[4]

Bishop Ithiel Clemmons, a historian for the Church of God in Christ, wrote, "The interrelatedness of holiness, spiritual encounter, and prophetic Christian social consciousness attracted people of all races to the Azusa Street revival. It was an egalitarian, ecumenical, interracial, interclass revival that for about three years defied the prevailing patterns of American life."[5]

A white preacher, G. B. Cashwell, excitedly traveled six days from Dunn, North Carolina, to Los Angeles to experience the Holy Spirit at Azusa Street and to receive the supernatural gift of speaking in tongues. But when he arrived, Minister Cashwell felt uncomfortable during the multiracial worship service. Although he wanted to receive this new spiritual gift, he didn't want a Black leader to lay hands on him so he could receive it. He turned to prayer to address the discomfort he felt.[6]

As he prayed, the Spirit of Love revealed the racism in his heart that was preventing him from receiving more of God's love and power. He had to choose: Would he submit to God, or would he submit to racism? Would he submit to being under the spiritual leadership and authority of the Black leaders at Azusa Street? Would he allow his Black Neighbors to come close physically and spiritually?

Ultimately, Minister Cashwell submitted to the Spirit of Love, and in turn, the Spirit of Love gave him new heart lenses. Society's dividing wall—which insisted he and his Black Neighbors remain separate and maintained he was in some way superior—fell in his heart. As Pastor Seymour laid hands on him, Minister Cashwell humbly received a rich spiritual gift through his Black Neighbor and spoke in tongues.[7]

Reflecting on the experience, Minister Cashwell noted that "a new crucifixion began in my life and I had to die to many things."[8] He remained at Azusa Street for several days. When he went back to North Carolina, he went with newfound intimacy with and honor for his Black Neighbor. The Spirit calling Minister Cashwell out was a loving invitation to go deeper into the heart of God and to see and love his Black Neighbor with new lenses.

So what about you? Is the Spirit lovingly calling you out for any racism in your heart? If so, how will you respond to the invitation to love with new lenses?

## PERNICIOUSNESS OF RACISM

The sin of racism—of seeing and treating your Black Neighbor without love because of their race—is a destructive, deadly force. An offhanded remark about your Black Neighbor's skin tone can sow death in her, just like putting on a KKK robe could. Regardless of its shape, racism is always destructive, and it's everywhere, like the air we breathe. Racism looks like . . .

- a Black person being complimented for being smart and articulate because they weren't expected to be
- a Black person being denied a job or promotion because they wear braids or another ethnic hairstyle
- segregated hair-care aisles at stores with "ethnic" and "regular" sections
- grocery stores in predominantly Black neighborhoods requiring customers to show their receipts when exiting the store
- neighborhoods with high Black populations receiving fewer home loans
- the creation of separate white churches and Black churches
- Black neighborhoods becoming "food deserts" because of a lack of fresh fruits and vegetables at grocery stores, while having a proliferation of unhealthy fast-food chains
- Band-Aids, crayons, and stockings labeled "flesh" color but coming in a singular peaches-and-cream shade
- #DrivingWhileBlack
- higher conviction rates and harsher sentencing for our Black Neighbors than our white neighbors who commit the same crimes
- trying to touch a Black woman's hair, like she's a pet

## Love Yourself: Be Humble and Question If You're Seeing Clearly

I grew up in the Church of God in Christ (COGIC), the Black-led Holiness Pentecostal denomination founded by Charles Harrison (C. H.) Mason, who was deeply influenced by the Azusa Street Revival. If you've spent a lot of time praying with COGIC folk, you know that some of them often pray some version of this prayer:

> Lord, please forgive me for anything I said, did, or thought that wasn't pleasing to you. Forgive me for any sins I committed knowingly or unknowingly. . . .

This prayer is imbued with humility. It assumes that we mess up often, despite our best efforts and despite not always knowing it. Cultivating this type of humility is essential as we interact with God and our Black Neighbor, because sometimes we just don't see ourselves. So when someone calls us out, we're baffled as to why because we don't see what they see. As author Ijeoma Oluo put it in *So You Want to Talk About Race,* our logical conclusion is "It just doesn't make sense to [me] so it cannot be right."[9] But sometimes our logical conclusion isn't right. When we pursue humility, we allow Love to give us new lenses.

A few years ago, a writing colleague, Melissa, and I started to become close friends. We worked at cafés together, talked about our writing dreams, and eventually talked about God. She described herself as spiritual but not Christian. So we chatted about God and faith, we prayed together, and she visited my church.

One day, she stopped coming to church and she stopped talking to me—a double whammy. She said I wasn't accepting of her and where she was in her life. I couldn't for the life of me understand what she was talking about. Of course, I wasn't a perfect friend—I mean, who is? But I couldn't grasp how someone I had been friends with for years—someone whom I had stood by and prayed for during some of the darkest times of her life—would just walk away. Because I couldn't understand her decision, I attributed her departure to not wanting to be around God or people who followed God. I didn't know what else to think. I grieved the loss of our friendship and kept praying that she would know God more deeply. I never thought to ask God to examine my heart lenses.

Several months later, I was praying when, seemingly out of nowhere, the Spirit showed me my heart toward Melissa. Yes, I loved her. Yes, I wanted the best for her, which included her fully embracing Jesus's love for her. But you know what else was in my heart? Impatience. The Spirit showed me that, deep down, I was kinda frustrated that Melissa was dragging her feet with Jesus. She was up and then down, in and then out, yes and then no. Because I didn't understand her approach to faith, when she said she felt like I wasn't accepting of her and where she was in her life, she was absolutely right. While praying in Love's presence, I saw how my impatience had caused her to not feel seen, loved, and valued right where she was.

Melissa was picking up on what was happening beneath the surface; she was talking about the state of my heart. I, however, was focused on my actions. My actions were great: praying for her, inviting her to church, taking her out to coffee. But the impurities in my heart—impatience and, if I'm honest, maybe a little bit of a desire to control—tainted my interactions with her.

Impurities may be standing between you and your Black Neighbor. Maybe one of your Black Neighbors has called you out for being proud or paternalistic. Or maybe you've been called out for saying or doing something racist, and you honestly don't see what they're talking about. In fact, maybe you've concluded that it's *their* issue or that they're just too sensitive. If this has happened, I wanna implore you to embrace "racial humility," a term coined by Professor Robin DiAngelo.[10] Essentially, racial humility means that you exercise humility when dealing with racial issues.

Honestly, I was hesitant to include the term in this book because I wanted to be able to say that humility is humility. If you're humble, then you're humble. If you're not, then you're not. No need to specify the type of humility, because humility is all-encompassing. But then I realized that while humility should be all-encompassing, when it comes to calling out racism especially when it's in our hearts, that's not often the case. The pervasiveness of racism on U.S. soil—particularly in the church—is so embedded in our foundations, so prolific in our practices, that we must counter it by practicing a specific, nuanced spiritual discipline: racial humility.

Overall, you can be someone who operates with a lot of humility, but you can still have some areas where you aren't very humble because you feel like they're non-issues. Ironically, these are the very areas you need the most humility in. Some Christians—especially white Christians—don't exercise racial humility because they don't believe they need to. It's a non-issue to them. And since they believe they're already humble and love everyone equally with the love of Christ, they often end up running into walls, doors, *and* their Black Neighbors!

Racial humility looks like taking the heart posture of COGIC folk and presuming you may have knowingly or unknowingly sinned against your Black Neighbor. Racial humility simply says, "Maybe I don't see things as clearly as I'd like to believe. Lemme listen to my Black Neighbor and the Spirit of Love to see if I need new lenses. Maybe they see more clearly than I do."

I'm so grateful that the Spirit showed me my heart toward

Melissa and then gave me new, patient lenses to see and love her through. I've since apologized and we've reconnected. I wish I'd had the humility to ask the Spirit about my heart lenses months before.

I know that in American culture, a racist is one of the worst things one can be labeled. But get this: In Scripture, pride is at the top of a list of seven sins God hates.[11] Racial humility is so crucial because it cuts against the pride God said is so detestable. Racial humility is the sinew that connects you to your Black Neighbor, because sometimes what severs your relationship with your Black Neighbor is not solely your racism but the pride that prevents you from acknowledging it. So if you get called out for saying or doing something racist, resist the urge to prove that your heart is good and that your eyesight is twenty-twenty. Instead, embrace humility. Wrap it around yourself like a cashmere blanket from Nordstrom.

## Love Yourself: Confess When You Don't See Your Black Neighbor Clearly

Several years ago, I met a white woman who oversaw DEI (diversity, equity, and inclusion) for her university. I started asking her questions about her work—cuz that's what I do, even while at dinner parties—and sensing my enthusiasm for the topic, she waxed poetic about the importance of DEI and her university's commitment to it. But at the end of our conversation, as she mentioned her school's affirmative action program, her mouth revealed what her heart really believed. When referring to the Black students admitted through this program, with shock in her voice, she said, "Some of them are really smart!"

*Did you catch that?* Her surprise that Black students could be smart? Her differentiation between the "smart" ones and the others? She didn't see her Black Neighbor as smart, capable, and worthy of a seat at her university's table. She viewed affirmative action programs as programs that brought in unqualified Black students to meet quotas and create diversity. And when I called her out, asking her what exactly she meant by her statement, she mumbled and fumbled her explanation. She couldn't explain it without admitting to her racist views. As she sat there, trying to protect her pride, she was actually missing an opportunity to experience this freeing truth: Confessing your racial sin allows love to cover your sin.

She could have said something like "What I said is jacked up. I'm really embarrassed. I'm so sorry." Now, I understand that hoping she would say that is a big ask. I understand that when someone gets called out for saying something racist, it's easier and perhaps instinctive to cover, not confess. Yet these uncomfortable moments are where humility is essential. If she were someone who was growing in humility, she would have asked me for forgiveness—if not in the moment, then definitely later on.

Had this DEI officer confessed and not covered, she could have experienced forgiveness from me in that moment when she felt exposed. Yes, I was offended by the statement—not to mention baffled as to how she became a DEI officer—but I also recognize that racism's sin-filled tentacles seek to suck the love out of our relationships with one another. Had she confessed, she would have experienced the love of God being poured out to her through me. But on that day, she missed out on the healing love that says, "I see what you just did, and I hold grace and forgiveness for you."

Beloved, forgiveness and love await you on the other side of confession. You don't have to cover your sins when you remember that "love covers a multitude of sins."[12] Knowing this, the next time your Black Neighbor or another neighbor calls you out, you can be free to confess and not cover. In fact, if you can remember a specific moment when you covered in the past, it's not too late to go back and ask for forgiveness. Your Black Neighbor will likely be shocked, and their respect for you will grow. Honesty is the bedrock of intimacy.

### *What to Do If You Get Called Out for Racism*

However painful, getting called out is a path toward heart transformation. If you live in a country that historically has routinely denigrated your Black Neighbor, then your heart most likely needs new lenses: new ways of seeing your Black Neighbor. So count it all joy when you're called out—either by a stranger or by your Black Neighbor whose cubicle sits next to yours. Be grateful that the Spirit of Love loves you too much to let you go through life running into walls and into your neighbors all the time.

But what happens when you're called out for racism? Bluntly? Directly? Or even with loving care? While every situation is different and may need a different response, here are some helpful steps to follow when you're called out for racism.

### 1. Listen

Don't try to justify what you did or said or why you did or said it. Just listen. Try to hear what the person is saying. Listen for their pain and hurt. Listen for their intent: Why are they telling you this? Are they trying to salvage your relationship? Help you grow?

### 2. Ask Questions

Tell them you want to fully understand; then ask if you can ask clarifying questions. If yes, then ask those questions. Try to avoid questions that start with "Why," as they can put people on the defensive, which is the *opposite* of what you want. Instead, use language like "Help me understand . . ." or "Can you go into more detail about . . ." Be kind and compassionate as you ask.

### 3. Apologize

After you've listened, apologize. Even if you don't fully understand what they're saying. Apologize. Resist the urge to try to prove that your heart vision is twenty-twenty. Instead, if you want to be really honest, say something like "I don't fully understand what you're saying, so I'm gonna need some time to think and process it. But I'm sorry I hurt you."

### 4. Examine Your Heart

Take the time to really think about and process what they said. Then examine your heart: Why did you say or do that thing? What was your intent? What was the impact on your Black Neighbor?

### 5. Ask the Spirit of Love to Examine Your Heart

Your heart can deceive you, and sometimes you can't see yourself clearly. In prayer, ask the Spirit to examine your heart. The Spirit will reveal the truth you couldn't see.

### 6. Ask a Trusted Friend to Join In on the Examination

If you feel like you still need clarity, then talk and pray with a trusted friend who listens to the Spirit. Choose a friend who regularly practices racial humility too. They may be able to help you figure out how to repair things with your Black Neighbor.

### 7. Return to the Person Who Called You Out to Further Discuss What Happened

Set up a time to continue the conversation. Enter the conversation with humility and love.

While you may not need to follow all seven every time you get called out for racism, these steps will help you cultivate humility before God and your Black Neighbor. Humility, when cultivated, softens our hearts and makes them pliable, able to bend toward another. Humility is always worth the steps. (Bonus: These steps will also cultivate humility if used when you're called out for *anything*!) When you humble yourself and allow others to examine your heart's eyes, you begin to create healthy relationships and close the gap between yourself and your Black Neighbor.

## Love Yourself: Persevere and Endure

My friend Kat is an avid salsa dancer who used to compete semi-professionally. When she was practicing for a competition in 2008, her dance partner lifted her into the air for a trick and somehow she fell on her head, right onto the hard ballroom floor. Thankfully, she was okay physically, but she was stunned and a bit traumatized.

After Kat calmed down, she instinctively knew that if she didn't try the move again, she would never be able to do lifts again because of fear. So she turned to her partner and said, "Let's try it again." And they did it. "Again!" she said, and they did it once more. They did the move again and again and again until the emotional sting of the fall dissipated from her memory.

Some of the most intense arguments I've ever experienced have centered on race. I've left some of those conversations bruised and injured, seething with hurt and anger, vowing to never experience that type of pain again. You might be like me: You were in a discussion—perhaps a workshop about race—when things went south. Accusations flew, tempers flared, and things got real ugly, real fast. You were bruised and injured, and you limped away stunned, vowing never to allow that to happen to you again.

If this describes you, then the Spirit of Love wants to bind up your wounds and pour love into the places of injury so they're no longer tender to the touch. Please don't allow past injuries to keep you hurt, fearful, angry, or bitter. Pray, and allow the Spirit to tend to unhealed racial injuries. You can't love your Black Neighbor well if you're injured or you lack endurance.

I've always hated running. When I had to run a mile in PE class to pass the Presidential Fitness Test, I literally huffed and puffed the entire time and was always one of the last stragglers to cross the finish line. After I graduated from high school, I never ran again. And I mean never. Not to get to the bank before it closed at 5 P.M. on Friday on a holiday weekend. Not even to grab the last five-dollar toaster at Target's Black Friday sale.

But then I tried salsa dancing. With salsa, you move on six of every eight beats, and if you're a woman, then the men love to twirl you again and again and again! The music is fast and pulsating. I absolutely love it.

One Friday night, several years ago, I went out dancing. I had been dancing for only about thirty minutes when I started to huff and puff. I looked around and noticed that the other women were twirling with loads of energy. That's when I realized that salsa dancing requires serious stamina. In order to dance with ease and enjoyment, I was going to have to build endurance by . . .

*Can you guess?*

By running.

So that's exactly what I did. Once or twice a week, I would run (slowly) around my neighborhood, including up and down a couple of hills. I hated running. I hated those hills. But I was determined to build the stamina I needed to dance. Building endurance wasn't easy, though. Sometimes I would be so out of breath that I had to walk or jog at a snail's pace, but I kept going. I wanted to dance with endurance. And enjoyment.

Likewise, if you want to love courageously again and again and again, through any falls and injuries, then you need a type of endurance that comes from the Spirit of Love.[13] One that enables you to love your Black Neighbors day after day, month after month, year after year, despite how tired you may feel. A love that endures even when your ego is bruised and humility tries to ghost you.

Seeing your own racial sin and the racial sins of your country over and over requires endurance. Also, struggling with the same sin repeatedly can be demoralizing. Over time, you can slip into either shame or denial. Endurance, however, will help you choose love after you run into (yet another) wall. Like my friend Kat, you will have the strength to keep doing the thing that once left you stunned and traumatized. You will gladly cultivate this endurance because you really love dancing—or, in this case, your Black Neighbor. And instead of vowing never to return to the dance floor, you will take the hand of your dance partner, Love, and say, "Again!"

You love yourself well when you choose to endure alongside Love instead of walking away from your neighbors because of either frustration or fatigue. Scripture consistently encourages us to persevere in our life with God. For example, one of the most famous passages, 1 Corinthians 13, reminds us that love "always perseveres."[14] Hebrews tells us to "throw off everything that hinders and the sin that so easily entangles" and to "run with perseverance the race marked out for us."[15] Another scripture encourages us to "not grow weary in doing good."[16]

Loving God takes endurance. Loving your neighbor takes endurance. Even loving yourself takes endurance! However, if you endure, Beloved, if you don't get tired of loving God, your Black

Neighbor, and yourself, then you will receive the greatest gift of all: life with God, forever.

Beloved, a forever life with God is predicated on allowing the Good Physician[17] to examine your eyes. So love yourself enough to go to the eye doctor. Receive all Love has for you and your Black Neighbor. I wonder how different your life might be if your goal wasn't to try to not be labeled racist. What if your goal was to be someone who humbly exchanged racism for love? What if you were someone who went around telling all your neighbors, "My lenses used to be no good. But look at these new lenses!" What if you were more celebratory of your present than ashamed of your past?

## Prayer Pause

I want to give you space to air out anything hidden in your heart. Fill in the prayer below either through the written word or by speaking out loud. After you've shared this with the Spirit of Love, share it with a trusted friend. Note: The trusted friend doesn't need to be your Black Neighbor. Please share with a Black Neighbor only if you strongly feel the Spirit asking you to.

*Spirit of Love,*
*I am not proud that I have thought . . .*
*I am embarrassed to say that . . .*
*I admit that I have . . .*
*Please grow me into someone who . . .*
*Please help me . . .*
*I forgive my Black Neighbor for . . .*
*I forgive myself for . . .*

# CHAPTER 2

# Robbed of Love

On a hot summer evening in August 2018, a middle-aged Black man lay unconscious on a train arriving at the Metro station in Long Beach, California. The Unconscious Man's right hand displayed a medical wristband, while his head revealed metal staples encrusted into his scalp. Passengers reported that he had vomited before passing out.

How do you think the passengers on the train responded to this Unconscious Man?

Although all of what happened on that Metro train isn't clear, one passenger captured part of it on camera. The filmed scene, as reported by Vibe,[1] was horrifying. When faced with a potentially life-threatening situation for his Black Neighbor, another passenger on the train—a white man dressed in a business suit—approached the Unconscious Man and dragged his limp body from the train onto the concrete platform outside. In the process, the Unconscious Man's genitals became exposed.

The businessman moved the unconscious Black man's body, not to administer care but to remove him from the train so it wouldn't be delayed. When chastised by a fellow passenger, the man rationalized his actions: "There are a lot of people on this train that have to get home."

The white passenger didn't hate his Black Neighbor. No, the businessman just didn't care about his Black Neighbor. Perhaps the Unconscious Man was nobody to him, someone of zero consequence. Maybe the businessman assumed the worst about the Unconscious Man's character. Maybe he assumed the man was a raging alcoholic or strung out on drugs. What's clear is that the businessman cared more about getting home on time than the man who might need lifesaving medical intervention.

Honestly, it's easy to chastise this passenger for his callous behavior, easy to imagine that we would've prioritized the Unconscious Man's needs over ours. But footage of the incident doesn't show any of the other passengers rushing to the man's aid either. In the video, they are seated and lob criticism at the businessman.

In Luke 10, Jesus told a story that suggests that we're more like the bystanders and businessman than we'd care to admit. In the familiar story famously known as "The Good Samaritan," Jesus illustrated that some of us—particularly those who claim to know and love God— would have looked past the Unconscious Man, even if we weren't emboldened to move his body. But Jesus didn't just use the story to call us out. He used the story to call us into a deeper love for our neighbor.

In Luke 10:25, we are introduced to an unnamed man who's referred to only as "an expert in the law." He was most likely an A+ religion student who became an expert and wanted everyone to *know* that he was an expert. Scripture says that this religion expert "stood up to test Jesus," which means he was pretty cocky because he thought he could go toe-to-toe with the Son of God.

"Teacher," he asked, "what must I do to inherit eternal life?"

Jesus, unfazed by his brazenness and in true OG style,* answered the man's question with a question.

---

* An OG is an original, someone highly respected. In some instances, an OG is an original gangster.

"What is written in the Law?" he replied. "How do you read it?"

He answered, "'Love the Lord your God with all your heart and with all your soul and with all your strength and with all your mind'; and, 'Love your neighbor as yourself.'"

After the religion expert finished, Jesus said, "You have answered correctly. Do this and you will live."

But the religion expert wouldn't leave it there. He asked, "And who is my neighbor?"[2]

Seems like a legitimate question on the surface, but it wasn't. The man "wanted to justify himself."[3] In other words, he asked the question because he wanted to *prove* that he was righteous. He wanted to prove that he was in good standing with God, one of the faithful "good guys." The religion expert was there not to learn from Jesus but to boast. Jesus answered his question, once again in OG style, with a story about a man who loved a stranger lavishly.

## Imagined Reading Exercise: The Robbed Man

The Good Samaritan story is a familiar one to many Christians. Whether you're familiar with this parable or it's new to you, I encourage you to read it slowly. In fact, don't read it like you would most stories. Instead, receive it in such a way that it can be absorbed into your heart, mind, and soul. I invite you to do what I call an imagined reading. Put yourself in the story—*imagine* and *feel* every aspect of it. Allow your senses to affect you. Pay close attention to anything you see, hear, feel, smell, or even taste. Read slowly, focusing on the details.

This first time, when you read the Good Samaritan parable, focus on the Robbed Man. If you're willing, imagine that you *are* him. What do you experience and feel throughout the story?

Resist the temptation to reach the end quickly; instead, live in the story, moment to moment. After you read the passage, take a few moments (or as much time as you need) to sit with the Robbed Man's/your feelings.

I recognize I'm asking you to immerse yourself in the story from the Robbed Man's perspective. I also realize this experience may be upsetting for some readers because the story contains violence and graphic scenes and can be triggering. You are loved; you are seen. Do what's best for you.

Before you begin, inhale a deep breath and exhale any expectations you may hold. Pause, inhale another deep breath, and release any desire to rush through this familiar story. Now, ask the Spirit of Love to impart this story to all of you.

*Spirit of Love, engage my heart, soul, mind, and strength during this imagined reading. Open up every part of me to receive the truth of this story. May I be dissuaded neither by the familiarity of the story nor by its magnitude. Remove anything that would prevent me from fully receiving the Word, and enfold me in your love.*

But he wanted to justify himself, so he asked Jesus, "And who is my neighbor?"

In reply Jesus said: "A man was going down from Jerusalem to Jericho, when he was attacked by robbers. They stripped him of his clothes, beat him and went away, leaving him half dead. A priest happened to be going down the same road, and when he saw the man, he passed by on the other side. So too, a Levite, when he came to the place and saw him, passed by on the other side. But a Samaritan, as he traveled, came where the man was; and when he saw him, he took pity on him. He went to him and bandaged his wounds, pouring on oil and wine. Then he put the man on his own donkey, brought him to an inn and took care of him. The next day he took out two denarii and gave them to the innkeeper. 'Look after him,' he said, 'and when I return, I will reimburse you for any extra expense you may have.'

"Which of these three do you think was a neighbor to the man who fell into the hands of robbers?"

The expert in the law replied, "The one who had mercy on him."

Jesus told him, "Go and do likewise."[4]

❧

*Reflect*
After reading the story, consider the questions below. Feel free to jot down your responses.

- What was stolen from the Robbed Man?
- How did the Robbed Man feel during the attack: physically, emotionally, psychologically, and spiritually?
- How long did he suffer from the attack? What were the long-term and short-term consequences of the robbery?
- How do you think he felt when the Good Samaritan cared for him so lavishly?

During my reflection, I imagined the Robbed Man traveling home, maybe having visited Jerusalem to worship at the temple there. This road was known for being curvy, dangerous, and often targeted by thieves. On the day before his assassination, Dr. Martin Luther King, Jr., described the road while preaching:

> It's a winding, meandering road. It's really conducive for ambushing. You start out in Jerusalem, which is about . . . 1200 feet above sea level. And by the time you get down to Jericho . . . you're about 2200 feet below sea level. That's a dangerous road.[5]

I imagined the fear the Robbed Man must've felt when he was outnumbered on this road by a pair or an entire gang of robbers overtaken by greed. I imagined that the first part of the attack was psychological: the Robbed Man sensing the danger, feeling trapped, and recognizing that he wouldn't fare well. But the robbers didn't stop at intimidation. They stripped him of his clothes—an inhumane act designed to strip away more than his attire—and stole all his possessions.

If the robbers had stopped there, it would have been bad enough. But they moved past intimidation and robbery; they beat the man. It was a brutal "insult to injury" transgression. Beating him until he was half-dead revealed the robbers' brutish character and ensured that the man would have no strength to recover his stolen goods. The Robbed Man was left on the side of the road, naked and unprotected from the heat and wind. He lay there, stripped of his dignity, subject to the mercy of whoever found him.

I started to cry during my imagined reading as the Robbed Man. My body clenched and my head throbbed through sobs. Instinctively, I switched from experiencing the passage in the first person, as if I were the Robbed Man, to experiencing it in the third person, as if I were witnessing it but not experiencing it personally. It was easier, emotionally and physically, to imagine the story this way. Once I noticed the switch, however, I forced myself back into the Robbed Man's shoes. But a minute later, I had again instinctively switched to the third person to separate myself from what I was experiencing.

Sensing a pattern, I asked God to help me stay in the story. The third time, I was able to imagine myself as the Robbed Man from the beginning to the end of the story. I imagined the in-between moments: The time he lay stretched out under the sun, first taking in gulps of air and then eventually only wisps. The moments he spent wondering if and when someone would take the time to come close. Did he hear the sandals of the priest and the Levite shuffle by? If he did, did he feel hope spring alive, only to die when the sandals shuffled to the other side? How did he endure the moments between the robbery and the repair, when he didn't know that the Spirit of Love already had plans to heal him?

I imagined the moment, too, when he realized that someone was clothing his nakedness, treating his wounds, and carrying him to safety. This same person was holding a cup of water to his mouth to relieve the parchedness. I imagined the relief he must have felt. The wave of emotions, the tears likely streaming down his face, and the safety the Robbed Man experienced in that moment. It reminded me of our Black Neighbor and the stony road he's trod from Africa to America.

## The Good Samaritan: Remix

The year was 1619. Benin, Ghana, and several others were feuding with their neighbor Niger. They knew that selling Niger could make them some money, so they sold him into slavery. Some of their people were sold into slavery, too—only this was a new type of slavery, one not practiced on African soil. Niger was captured, beaten, starved, and shipped to the other side of the world. He lost his language, his culture, his land.

In the new land, he was deemed less than a person. A thing. Eventually three-fifths of a person when his enslavers plotted to win an election. For centuries, Niger and his descendants would lie broken, bruised, and beaten, separated from their homeland, their language, their tribes, and their families and, of course, always separated from the owners of the new land they tilled. This separation lasted even after their bodies were released from their physical chains; this separation still exists.

One day, one of Niger's descendants lay on this American soil, shackled, on the side of a nondescript road, half-dead, gasping for life. Like his father, grandfather, great-grandmother, and ancestors before them, this Robbed Man had been attacked by robbers, stripped of his clothes and identity, beaten down in every way a person can be beaten.

And when a pastor saw him, in pain and in shackles, the pastor walked away and said he didn't need to intervene because it didn't matter if the man's body was bruised and shackled, as long as his soul was saved.

And when a small-group Bible study leader saw Niger's descendant, bound and in need of care, the small-group leader walked away, saying it wasn't his place to interfere. Slaves should obey their masters, he argued, adding that it was a sin to disobey Scripture.

Centuries later, relatives of the American pastor and Bible study leader, along with their distant cousins from Great Britain and Great Britain's neighbors in France, Germany, Portugal, and Belgium, returned to Niger's homeland in Africa.

They came neither to apologize nor to restore parts of what

their ancestors had stolen. They returned instead to pillage the land again, this time for its natural resources. During the Berlin Conference of 1884–85, leading European nations carved up the continent of Africa like an animal in an illegal butcher shop. They dismembered it so they could control it with their gunpowder and might. Bloodied, battered, and beaten, the land limped along for decades, still hemorrhaging from the multi-century massacre, still not fully in control of its soil or its citizens. While Africa's scattered descendants still struggled to make paper homes on distant shores, its remaining residents lay subject to domination and destitution in their own land. Many historians call this the Scramble for Africa. A more accurate name is the Great Robbery.

Worldwide, the effects of that robbery are still visible. In fact, the robbery continues to this day through racism, discrimination, underfunded schools, segregated neighborhoods, unfair legal practices, pay disparities, inequitable healthcare, and much more. Niger's descendants deserve much better.

So where is the Good Samaritan? Where are the people who will face the bruises and brokenness head on and come close? Who will tend to the wounds and pain of Niger's descendants? Who will love lavishly, despite the personal costs?

Through the Good Samaritan story, Jesus gave us a beautiful example of the love that should flow between neighbors. While this story may be thousands of years old, the message rings true today. We are called to love the Robbed Man—our Black Neighbor— amid the devastating generational robbery he has experienced. Jesus didn't ask us to sit on the sidelines and watch; he didn't tell us to walk on the other side of the road and avoid the pain. No, he called us into a lavish, full, multidimensional, and beautiful love for our Black Neighbor, the impact of which can transcend generations. Will you accept his invitation?

## HEART CHECK

- When you read and hear alarming statistics and stories about your Black Neighbor, how do you usually respond? Do you look for ways to love, or do you think that they should just work harder?

- Identify three specific ways your Black Neighbor has been robbed. What would it feel like to imagine yourself in those same situations? Resist any urge to separate your emotions from the experiences.

- What impact would those robberies have on your life today? What impact would they have on your family's lives?

### Prayer Pause

*Spirit of Love, please help me open all of myself—my heart, soul, mind, and strength—to my Black Neighbor whose experiences mirror those of the Robbed Man. Help me truly see and feel the ways he's been robbed and continues to be robbed. Help me love my Black Neighbor as myself.*

Note: If you feel a little spent after reading this chapter, feel free to take a walk, write your thoughts, and return when you're ready. Peace and blessings over you!

# CHAPTER 3

# Love Withheld

I remember the first time I saw a dead body. I was at the funeral of one of my fourth-grade classmates, William, who had died from a rare form of cancer. I'm not sure how much I understood death at nine years old, but when I looked at his lifeless body, I felt the power of death: its ability to ravage a physical body and leave gutting grief and destruction in its wake.

The 1991 film *Boyz n the Hood* showed a group of young Black children like me seeing a dead body for the first time. In one scene, a young boy asks his three friends, "Y'all wanna see a dead body?" The group then walks to a field where their Black Neighbor, a young Black man, lies deserted. The kids peek down, curious. The ghastly scene is their first up-close-and-personal look at death but definitely not their last.[1]

The 1990s birthed a proliferation of inner-city movies that portrayed death and robbery via violence in South L.A. and beyond. Movies like *Menace II Society, Dead Presidents,* and *Set It Off* sparked debates nationwide: Who or what was responsible for the theft and violence experienced by our Black Neighbors in many inner-city communities? Was it the faction of our Black Neighbors who were willing to climb out of poverty by any means necessary, even if it included robbery and mayhem? Was it the dangerous road that made it easy for them to be robbed and denied a fair shot? Or was it every non-Black neighbor who walked by them on that same road yet did nothing to help?

Some film and cultural critics questioned if these films were even necessary, asking if they were glorifying violence or, just as egregiously, seeming to confirm what American culture already preached about its Black Neighbors: that we are dangerous and somehow deserving of every bad thing we have experienced.

While critics rightly questioned the impact of these movies, by and large the general public overlooked the road's blighted condition as portrayed in the films. Resultantly, our neighbors continued to walk past us, never thinking to stop.

In the Good Samaritan story, the priest and the Levite walked right past the Robbed Man. Did they avoid him because they assumed he was dead? Were they dodging the gravitas of death, or was something else at play? Why did they refuse to come close?

## Imagined Reading Exercise: The Priest and the Levite

Let's review the passage in Luke 10. This time, imagine that you are the priest and the Levite. Put yourself in their sandals. Where do you think the priest and the Levite were coming from? Where do you think they might have been going?

Before you begin, inhale a deep breath and exhale completely. Pause; inhale and exhale another deep breath. Allow yourself to slow down. Use the prayer below or craft your own.

*Spirit of Love, I invite your love inside me. Would you show me any ways I'm tempted to withhold love from my Black Neighbor? Would you reveal any excuses I use to withhold love?*

Once again, do your best to live in the story moment to moment as the priest and the Levite. At the end of the passage, take some time to reflect.

But he wanted to justify himself, so he asked Jesus, "And who is my neighbor?"

In reply Jesus said: "A man was going down from Jerusalem to Jericho, when he was attacked by robbers. They stripped him of his clothes, beat him and went away, leaving him half dead. A priest happened to be going down the same road, and when he saw the man, he passed by on the other side. So too, a Levite, when he came to the place and saw him, passed by on the other side. But a Samaritan, as he traveled, came where the man was; and when he saw him, he took pity on him. He went to him and bandaged his wounds, pouring on oil and wine. Then he put the man on his own donkey, brought him to an inn and took care of him. The next day he took out two denarii and gave them to the innkeeper. 'Look after him,' he said, 'and when I return, I will reimburse you for any extra expense you may have.'

"Which of these three do you think was a neighbor to the man who fell into the hands of robbers?"

The expert in the law replied, "The one who had mercy on him."

Jesus told him, "Go and do likewise."[2]

✿

*Reflect*

After you've completed your reading, please consider these questions:

- Why did the priest and the Levite pass by on the other side? Why not stay on the same side of the road as the Robbed Man?
- What didn't they want to confront or see up close?
- What thoughts may have gone through the priest and the Levite's heads? Which emotions could they have been feeling?
- Why didn't they have pity on the Robbed Man like the Good Samaritan?

🌢

## The Stench of Death

To fully understand the priest's and the Levite's reactions, we need to learn more about Jewish religious law. The law contains clear mandates about separating the pure things of God from impure things. In biblical times, dead bodies or anything associated with death was rendered impure, or unclean, and couldn't come into the holy temple—God's pure resting place.[3] While everyone was commanded to cleanse themselves when exposed to any impure things, priests were under even stricter regulations because they worked in the temple.

Levites were responsible for leading public worship, so they served various roles, from working as guards at the temple to leading people in chanting the psalms. Priests were Levites with an elevated status. They were the only people allowed inside the inner parts of the temple, the parts considered most sacred, and they were responsible for receiving the people's offerings to God, which included the sin offering* and the guilt offering.†

Priests were prohibited from coming into contact with dead bodies, with the exception of their close relatives.[4] If priests came into contact with a dead body, then, according to Jewish law, it would make them ceremonially unclean. They would be unable to resume their duties at the temple until they were ceremonially clean again: a process that spanned seven days, involved washing their clothes and body, and required a sprinkling of purification water.[5] In the interim, priests were social pariahs, shunned because anyone or anything they touched would also be labeled unclean. For priests and Levites, uncleanness was easily transmitted from one person to the next, kind of like Ebola or even COVID-19.

So when the priest avoided the Robbed Man, was it because he didn't want to endure the costs of uncleanness if the man was dead? If so, did the priest not want to be inconvenienced for a stranger? Or was it more than that: Did the priest think his job at the temple was more important than tending to a person who might be dying? Or perhaps he didn't want to be shunned for uncleanness, by both the other priests he worked alongside and the people he led?

Although the priest was under stricter purification regulations

---

* The sin offering was made when someone sinned unintentionally and later realized their guilt. Leviticus 4 and Numbers 15:22–29 offer details, if you'd like to learn more. Warning: The descriptions of the offerings are pretty graphic, thus illustrating the severity of our sin against God.

† The guilt offering was offered when a person either violated God's holy things or violated another person. The violator had to bring an offering plus a financial gift as reparations. Please see Leviticus 5:14–6:7 for details.

than the Levite, both men had the same response. They "passed by on the other side." They chose not to endure the inconvenience either of having to be cleansed if the Robbed Man were in fact dead or of caring for him if he were still alive. They chose convenience and the comfort of their religious and social standing over the Robbed Man's well-being, and the priest used religious protocol to shield himself from any neighborly responsibility.

Today you might be tempted to avoid coming close to your Black Neighbor as an ally on the road for fear of what that association will cost you socially and personally. While there's no official caste system in the U.S., there is a social hierarchy wherein Black folks have been kicked to the bottom and told it's their fault. Choosing to sit with your Black Neighbor amid death-inducing robbery will incite reproach.

In the 1960s, a small fraction of white citizens marched and protested alongside their Black Neighbors. Today we label them "civil rights activists," but they were just ordinary people who chose to *stand up* against the robbery their Black Neighbors were experiencing. When they stood up, they were yelled at, ridiculed, and spat on. These white allies experienced stares and jeers from society, friends, and even family members. Unlike the priest and the Levite, these allies came close and, as a result, became social pariahs because they dared to topple the system of segregation that insisted they were somehow superior.

As you choose to align yourself with your Black Neighbor, some folks whom you considered friends and even some family members may question why you're bothering to love. They may ask why you're putting so much effort into loving your Black Neighbor and not all neighbors. They may insist that saying "Black Lives Matter" is divisive and maintain that saying "All Lives Matter" is better, because they don't understand the origins of the former. They may insist that our country's racial sins (slavery, Jim Crow, segregation, redlining, etc.) are just relics of our past that have no bearing on our present. In fact, some of your friends and family will *blame* your Black Neighbor for their robbery: *Why was he out in the middle of the night? Why didn't he just talk to the men calmly? Why didn't she use a turn signal to avoid being pulled over?* They may even try comparing apples to oranges: *My family came to this country with nothing, and we've done just fine.* Or they may blatantly say, *Well, things would be different if they just worked harder.*

Some may even ridicule you for stopping and potentially risking your own safety. Bystanders—or, in the case of the parable, *by-walkers*—see the Robbed Man, then say, "Maybe the robbers are waiting to attack whoever decides to help," as they move to the other side. Beloved, don't listen to them! They have much to learn about the ways of Love.

By assuming that the Robbed Man was dead and maintaining distance, the priest and the Levite circumvented having to witness his pain up close. They also circumvented the suffering they'd endure while witnessing his trauma. On an emotional level, I can understand why the Levite and the priest may not have wanted to be loaded down by the Robbed Man's circumstances.

As a journalist, I interviewed sexual assault survivors for a news story at the onset of the #MeToo movement. After hearing story after story of women in the entertainment industry who had been assaulted, I found myself curled up in a ball on my bed, heaving sobs over experiences that weren't mine. I was dealing with secondhand trauma—an experience by someone who witnesses or hears about another person's trauma.

Trauma is heavy for those who've experienced it firsthand *and* those who find themselves in the wake of its destruction. But avoiding pain and trauma should never be our goal. Instead, love should be our goal, and our perfect example is no further than the cross.

God saw us in our broken, robbed state, but he didn't just walk by on the other side of the road. No, he came close in the person of Jesus. When Jesus died on the cross, he didn't only carry our sins. He lifted our trauma and pain onto his shoulders and carried them to his grave. Just as the Spirit of Love raised Jesus from the dead, so too can the Spirit help us come close to our Black Neighbors by expanding and strengthening our hearts to hold gut-wrenching pain.*

Are you tempted to either see or read about the pain of your Black Neighbor without allowing it to make an impact on you? Are you quick to go about your day as if nothing ever happened for fear of being weighed down emotionally and maybe even experiencing secondhand trauma? If you do, then like the priest and the Levite, in circumventing your Black Neighbor, you're circumventing your opportunity to serve.

## OTS

I was a camper at Campus by the Sea, a Christian camp on Catalina Island that regularly hosts up to 250 college students. During their stay, each camper was asked to volunteer in some capacity. We lovingly referred to it as an "opportunity to serve" (OTS). The opportunities to serve included shoveling dirt, painting cabins, and any other laborious tasks on the grounds.

* We also know that counseling and therapy are essential tools for dealing with trauma and pain. Countless counselors are available to serve you, many of whom are Christian, if that's what you prefer, and many of whom are covered by your health insurance provider, if you have insurance.

One of the more regular OTSs revolved around meals. The camp was responsible for cooking up mounds of food at breakfast, lunch, and dinner for all the students and staff members. As you can imagine, the prep, setup, service, and teardown for each meal was intense, so staffers would regularly ask for help. Before each meal, the OTS-involved campers arrived fifteen minutes early to set up plates, cups, and silverware. While OTS was a requirement for all campers, no one ever checked to see if you did it. If you didn't show up, then the other campers scheduled to serve before that meal would simply fill the need without you.

There were two types of campers: those who truly saw OTS as an opportunity to serve their fellow campers, even if they ended up with the 7:30 A.M. breakfast slot, and those who saw it as an opportunity to suffer. Perhaps *suffer* is an extreme description, but some campers preferred sleeping in, having fun with their friends, or just finding a quiet space to introvert instead of serving. They skipped their OTS, or if they showed up, they did it while grumbling, "Why do we have to do this? I wish I were kayaking instead . . ."

Both groups of campers received the same invitation from the camp leaders. The only difference was how they viewed it and thus experienced it.

The same was true for the priest, the Levite, and the Good Samaritan. They all had the same opportunity to serve the Robbed Man as he lay on the side of the road, but the priest and the Levite interpreted it as a grim opportunity to suffer and said, "No, thanks. I'm good!"

When Jesus used these two religious leaders as negative examples of what it means to love our neighbor, he emphasized that love takes precedence over everything, including religious obligations. The crux of all Jewish laws is loving God and loving one's neighbor.

The priest and the Levite did neither, because their hearts never transitioned from duty to desire. They remained more concerned about what tending to the Robbed Man might cost them than what the Robbed Man might gain. To them, the cost of love was too high. The cost of not loving, though, was higher.

## When We Choose Not to See

In the spring of 2019, I was in San Francisco, California, being honored as part of the Emerging Leaders Fellowship through ARC, a non-profit organization dedicated to supporting creatives whose art sits at the intersection of faith and culture. I was walking down the hill next to the church where our conference was taking place when I spotted an Unhoused Black Woman in her fifties dressed in tattered clothes. She sat on the grass adjacent to where another conference attendee and I were passing. I ignored the woman and kept walking. The woman walking next to me, however, stopped to ask our Black Neighbor how she was doing. I stopped too. The conversation was brief. The Unhoused Woman simply smiled, said that she was well, and didn't ask us for anything.

As we walked farther down the hill, I kept thinking about how I initially ignored the Unhoused Woman, how I didn't really *see* her. At first, I tried to justify myself, thinking that this situation was an outlier. There were plenty of times I had stopped to buy food for my Unhoused Neighbors. Looking back now, I realize that it's not just that I didn't really see the woman. It's that I didn't really *want* to see her. If I'm honest, I subconsciously believed that I was more important than the woman and that my schedule was more important than her particularly visible problems. To me, she was in a different category of people: those not worthy of my time and attention.

Had I not been so engrossed in my conversation, so concerned about being on time to my next meeting, had I taken more time with her, then I would have *seen* more of the Unhoused Woman; my heart would have *felt* more for her. I may have prayed for her and asked if she needed anything. The Spirit of Love may have filled an unspoken need through me. Who knows what else could have transpired had I only come in close to her?

The sobering reality is that besides not loving her in that moment, the latent lens of pride remained, which kept me from acknowledging the hierarchical lens I viewed her through. Both lenses blocked love, and if I did it to her without thinking, surely I would do it again to someone else without thinking. I had missed my opportunity to serve—to be the hands and feet of Jesus to her.

What about you? Does your current lens allow you to *really* see your Black Neighbor? Do you even *want* to see the ways your Black Neighbor has been robbed and left on the side of the road to fend for herself? Do you think that you and your schedule are more important than your Black Neighbor's needs? Beloved, when we choose to avoid intimacy with our Black Neighbors, we are robbed of more than the opportunity to love our neighbor and "do the right thing." We are robbed of a divine experience that can come only through the outpouring of love.

In the parable, the priest and the Levite were robbed of experiencing the Spirit of Love pour through them into the Robbed Man. They missed out on the intimacy that would've formed between them and the Robbed Man as they served him in his most vulnerable state. The priest and the Levite didn't understand that loving him at his greatest point of pain was a grand opportunity for them to witness the resurrection of both the Robbed Man's pain and the decaying parts of their hearts.

While the two religious leaders avoided contamination from a dead body, they entombed their hearts in fear and selfishness—types of death. They created a fence that robbed them of an experience where love and life could grow.

Had the priest and the Levite drawn close to the Robbed Man, their hearts would've been clean. Had they suffered with the Robbed Man, their love would've grown and ultimately produced life in them! Their love for and service to their neighbor would've mirrored their love for and service to God. The Spirit of Love would've flowed through them to the Robbed Man. But the priest and the Levite didn't choose to bathe the Robbed Man in love; he remained bathed in robbery, repudiation, and death. And so did they.

In this story, Jesus revealed that true uncleanness is internal, not external. He illustrated that although these two religious leaders weren't willing to become unclean, he was. Jesus was foreshadowing the type of love that he was birthing into the earth—he would become sin in order to defeat sin and the death it produces.[6] He would bridge the divide to come up close and personal to our sins, cleanse us from them, and free us from death.

Jesus invited the people into a love that superseded religious regulations. A love that removed the shroud of death and experienced the light of resurrection. He extends the same invitation to us today.

Beloved, when you love your Black Neighbor, you allow God to change your vision so that you see your neighbor—particularly one who's been stripped and robbed or left for dead either physically, psychologically, or financially—the way God does. You see him as a beloved child, made in God's image. Ultimately, you get to see yourself in him. Your vision shifts so you don't turn your head away either because of discomfort or because you don't want to be inconvenienced. Instead, God enables you to truly *see* and *feel*.

## HEART CHECK

- When have you been tempted to act like the priest and the Levite?

- In what area of your life is the Spirit of Love inviting you to release the fear of experiencing pain and trauma?

- In what area of your life are you hesitant to accept the opportunity to serve your Black Neighbor?

- What types of death inside you do you need God to cleanse?

### *Prayer Pause*

*Spirit of Love, I need your help to love my Black Neighbor the way you love them. When I see their injuries, help me not to walk by for any reason, including any fears of how I might be affected emotionally or socially. Help me not to blame my Black Neighbor for their injuries. Give me a love that isn't afraid to come close.*

# CHAPTER 4

# Love Poured Out

Love isn't love till you've given it away.
—"Love Isn't Love" by Commissioned

My heart was melting. Joey, my then two-year-old godson, was eating a favorite snack: milk and cookies. I walked over to the kitchen table to sit next to him. As I brushed his thin black hair away from his eyes, he looked up at me with a crumbled cookie in hand, cheesed big, and loudly exclaimed, "Chanté God-Mah, I love you!"

He had never declared his love for me before, and I stood stunned as teeny-tiny wells filled my eyes. "I love you, too, Joey," I responded.

Later that evening, I wondered how his two-year-old self defined love. *Does Joey even know what love is?* He was still so young to grasp the depths of love, but he was beginning to learn what it was and how to express it, something we all did when we were kids.

One of the first Bible verses I memorized in children's church was John 3:16: "For God so loved the world that he gave his one and only Son, that whoever believes in him shall not perish but have eternal life." As a kid, I didn't understand the depths of this scripture, but as an adult, I recognize that it's a description and illustration of multidimensional love. Because God *loved,* God *gave.*

Love *gives.* Love gives completely; love gives unreservedly. Love gives physically, emotionally, and spiritually. Love is expansive and all-encompassing. Jesus knew the depths of love, so when he said to love our neighbor, he knew he had to give an example of what that looks like.

## Imagined Reading Exercise: The Good Samaritan, aka the Love Samaritan

We're gonna wrap up our immersion in the Good Samaritan story by looking at it from the perspective of its namesake. How did he demonstrate a multidimensional, Godlike love?

To prepare, please take a moment to breathe and invite the Spirit of Love to sit with you. Inhale a deep breath and exhale fully. Pause, take another deep breath, and release any desire to rush through this story. Now, ask the Spirit of Love to impart this story to you so that you can understand it holistically. Feel free to either use the prayer below or craft your own.

*Spirit of Love, please give me eyes to see this passage anew. Please remove any reservations that may emerge as I read. Please enlarge my heart so that it can receive and release the multidimensional love that's illustrated in this story.*

Next I invite you to review the Good Samaritan story again as an imagined reading. This time, imagine that you are the Good Samaritan, whom I'm renaming the Love Samaritan because love is his essence. Once again, do your best to live in the story moment to moment. Take your time; then at the end of the passage, spend a few moments reflecting.

But he wanted to justify himself, so he asked Jesus, "And who is my neighbor?"

In reply Jesus said: "A man was going down from Jerusalem to Jericho, when he was attacked by robbers. They stripped him of his clothes, beat him and went away, leaving him half dead. A priest happened to be going down the same road, and when he saw the man, he passed by on the other side. So too, a Levite, when he came to the place and saw him, passed by on the other side. But a Samaritan, as he traveled, came where the man was; and when he saw him, he took pity on him. He went to him and bandaged his wounds, pouring on oil and wine. Then he put the man on his own donkey, brought him to an inn and took care of him. The next day he took out two denarii and gave them to the innkeeper. 'Look after him,' he said, 'and when I return, I will reimburse you for any extra expense you may have.'

"Which of these three do you think was a neighbor to the man who fell into the hands of robbers?"

The expert in the law replied, "The one who had mercy on him."

Jesus told him, "Go and do likewise."[1]

❧

*Reflect*
- What do you think "he took pity on him" means?
- How did the Love Samaritan bathe the Robbed Man with love?
- What did the Love Samaritan sacrifice and risk to show love to the Robbed Man?

What the Love Samaritan did in this story is so G* that I want to break it down moment by moment. Let's start when he first saw the Robbed Man.

When he saw him . . . he went to him.

When the Love Samaritan saw the Robbed Man, he neither allowed himself to stay distant nor created more distance. Instead, he came closer. That word "saw" has multiple meanings in the original Greek language and can refer to visual sight or a deeper kind of seeing. When the story says that he saw the Robbed Man, another way to interpret the word is to say that he experienced him.[2] In other words, he felt the Robbed Man's condition with his heart. He took the Robbed Man and his beaten state into himself. His experience of the Robbed Man compelled him to respond with love and honor. His compassion for the man only increased as he came closer.

---

* "G" is short for "gangster," and it can have a good connotation, showing that someone exudes strength and fearlessness.

The priest and the Levite briefly saw the Robbed Man, but they chose not to come close and *experience* him. They embraced distance. The Love Samaritan, however, embraced intimacy with his neighbor by going to him. The same can be true for us as we ask ourselves how close we're willing to get.

If you see your Black Neighbor injured, then how do you console them? If you live close by, do you visit just for a few minutes while you drop off a homemade casserole or forego visiting altogether and instead organize a fundraiser on GoFundMe from the comfort of your computer screen? In other words, do you find ways to serve that distance you from their pain? Or do you willingly and purposefully draw close and stay close? Do you respond like the Love Samaritan and choose intimacy?

He took pity on him.

After the Love Samaritan saw the Robbed Man, "he took pity on him." Being pitied isn't something many Americans aspire to, as it can carry a connotation of weakness and American culture celebrates strength over weakness all day, every day. But that phrase actually means "to have the bowels yearn, i.e. (figuratively) feel sympathy."[3] Let's keep it all the way real and acknowledge that when your bowels are moving, your body has no choice but to acquiesce! You stop whatever you're doing and pay attention to what your bowels are saying—*you feel me?*

In this context, taking pity on someone is being so overwhelmed with compassion that you can't help but help. It ain't optional, because your insides are in charge. I call it *inevitable compassion* because action is unavoidable. This type of compassion overflows from the multidimensional love we experience with God.

The Love Samaritan had inevitable compassion. When he took pity on the Robbed Man, his bowels were yearning. He was feeling an intense sympathy, and his body moved in response. Beloved, the Spirit of Love wants to give you this type of compassion for your Black Neighbor so your heart and body instinctively bend in service.

He . . . bandaged his wounds, pouring on oil and wine.

After the Love Samaritan saw and took pity on the Robbed Man, he tended to the man personally. He bent down and examined the wounds, treated them, examined the wounds again, and treated them some more. He experienced a physical and emotional intimacy that a nurse would with a patient. But the Love Samaritan gave even more. He gave his personal resources—the oil and wine. Physically, the wine served as an antiseptic, and the oil soothed the inflammation. Spiritually, the wine symbolized God's lavishness and abundance being poured into the Robbed Man's pain, and the oil symbolized the Holy Spirit's presence with him.[4] The Love Samaritan embodied God's physical and spiritual care for the man.

Let's remember the Robbed Man's injuries weren't a quick fix. He had been beaten within an inch of his life, the wounds were severe, and bandaging them would take time and patience. Given the Robbed Man's extensive injuries, the Love Samaritan could easily have felt overwhelmed or discouraged by the long healing process. He needed to have *compassionate long-suffering,* love that is demonstrated and fought for over the long haul.

*Compassionate long-suffering* ain't for the faint of heart. As I write this chapter, my aunt Jackie is battling cancer. She is undergoing intensive treatment that makes it painful for her to walk. "Look!"

she says, with an almost childlike awe, as she peels away dead skin from the heels of her feet.

I would sometimes see her via FaceTime when our family gathered for our prayer calls, but I didn't understand the detrimental effects of her treatment until I stayed at her house for a week, where I saw the effects up close and personal. The camera hadn't revealed that her nose, toes, feet, and fingernails were blackening. Sitting next to her on the couch, I saw the extent of the damage the cancer-killing treatment had done to her entire body.

Always the jokester, one morning she tried to show the family the charred parts of her body, not to build empathy but to kinda gross us out. Plus, I imagine, to somehow lighten the load. But seeing the parts of her that once were fully alive and active now fighting for life felt too painful to witness. We instinctively turned our heads away and asked her to end the macabre show-and-tell presentation. She persisted, insisting that we see. At that moment, I caught myself not wanting to experience her pain with her. It was too potent.

Pain and death can be overwhelming. As human beings, we have a natural aversion and scurry away because we weren't made for death. But, like the Love Samaritan, I believe we can hold pain and every type of death rightly when the Spirit of Love undergirds us.

When we acknowledge that the injuries to our Black Neighbors are not solely individual but rather collective, then we can recognize that quick fixes won't effectively treat these wounds. They are generational, going back hundreds of years, back to 1619. In the groundbreaking (and controversial) book *Post Traumatic Slave Syndrome,* Dr. Joy DeGruy wrote about the collective injuries our Black Neighbors have faced while on U.S. soil: "Post Traumatic Slave Syndrome is a condition that exists when a population has experienced multigenerational trauma resulting from centuries of slavery and continues to experience oppression and institution-alized racism today. Added to this condition is a belief (real or imagined) that the benefits of the society in which they live are not accessible to them."[5]

In light of this multigenerational trauma, the long journey toward restoration will no doubt span many generations. But if we're willing, the Spirit will grow compassionate long-suffering in us for our Black Neighbors so we can stand with them as Love pours wine over their pain and oil over their wounds, granting us and our neighbors the strength of a love that endures and deepens over time.

> Then he put the man on his own donkey, brought him to an inn and took care of him.

After the Love Samaritan cared for the Robbed Man's wounds, he lifted the man onto his own animal for transport. The Love Samaritan delayed his plans, however important, so that he could care for the man in a safe place. The Love Samaritan didn't just give money to the Robbed Man; he gave himself. There was a transfer of his *being* into the Robbed Man. By offering his time and material resources, the Love Samaritan poured out God's love for the Robbed Man. He became a conduit of God's love.

The transferred love was an integral part of the Robbed Man's healing process because he didn't just experience the loss of money and mobility. During the beating and stripping, he was subjected to hurt, harm, selfishness, brutality—all enemies of love. What he needed, just as much as physical bandages and shelter, were spiritual bandages and shelter. What he needed, just as much as physical restoration, was soul restoration. The Robbed Man needed to be wrapped and sheltered in a multidimensional love that bathed him physically, emotionally, psychologically, relationally, financially, and spiritually. He needed a love with divine roots.

The Spirit of Love holds the same kind of love for your Black Neighbor and invites you to become a conduit of this multidimensional love. If you want to become a conduit, then regularly spend time in prayer, sit with Scripture, and ask God to endow you with love for your Black Neighbor. As you do, you'll grow a love with divine roots.

> The next day he took out two denarii and gave them to the innkeeper. "Look after him," he said, "and when I return, I will reimburse you for any extra expense you may have."

The Love Samaritan stayed with the Robbed Man, presumably nursing his wounds throughout the night. When he departed, he left about two days' worth of wages at the inn. I want you to take a moment to think about how much money you make in two working days. *That's* how much money the Love Samaritan left for the man's care. Out of love, he assumed responsibility for his neighbor. To him, it was a privilege and an honor. His neighbor's need was his opportunity to serve. Likewise, we have the opportunity to serve our Black Neighbors through our love-rich resources. Our "oil and wine" are gifts from God that we can pour over our Black Neighbors.

Eventually the Love Samaritan had to leave to tend to his personal and professional obligations, so he asked the innkeeper to look out for the Robbed Man and promised to return with more money. The instructions he gave to the innkeeper revealed the depth of his love for the Robbed Man and are a model for how we can interact with our Black Neighbor.

First, the Love Samaritan asked the innkeeper, a person within close physical proximity to the Robbed Man, to care for him. The Love Samaritan could've easily justified leaving without securing another caregiver, saying, "I've done my part. I delayed my plans, nursed the man, and paid for his lodging. He should be *fine* from here on out." Instead, the Love Samaritan took an even stronger stand for the man by telling the innkeeper to care for him as well.

Equally noteworthy is that the Love Samaritan wasn't just concerned with the Robbed Man's immediate well-being. When he told the innkeeper that he'd return with additional resources, he was taking responsibility for the Robbed Man's future well-being as well! If this were a sermon and I were a Black preacher, this is the part where I'd yell, "Turn to your neighbor and say, 'ABOVE and BEYOND! ABOVE and BEYOND!'"

The Love Samaritan was committed to the man's well-being over time. And remember, the Robbed Man was a stranger to him! He wasn't fueled by any long-standing relationship with the man. Love and love alone fueled his concern over the long haul. His love, his generosity, his ability to come close to death and pain, came solely through the Spirit of Love.

The only way to love like the Samaritan is to be infused with the Spirit of Love. The Samaritan's inevitable compassion, compassionate long-suffering, and multidimensional love came from the Spirit because God *is* love. He was able to love the Robbed Man so fully because he had already received this love from God. The Samaritan allowed God's love to flow from him to the Robbed Man. In doing so, he and the Robbed Man experienced the fuller, multidimensional love of God.

Beloved, that's exactly how you get to love your Black Neighbor: from the love God has already planted in your heart for you. When you experience God's love flowing to you and growing inside you, then God's love can flow through you to your Black Neighbor. The beautiful thing about love is that, when allowed to flow freely, it never runs out. As love flows through you, it grows, so the more love you give, the more you're able to receive. And the more love you receive, the more you can give.

Open your heart, and ask God to infuse you with love for your Black Neighbor. Receive the full experience of love that God has for you and for your neighbor. If your prayer is sincere, I promise you'll receive what you ask for.[6]

## An Invitation to Love

At the end of Jesus's story, he asked the religion expert "Which of these three do you think was a neighbor to the man who fell into the hands of robbers."[7] The expert was no fool. He knew that the Love Samaritan, "the one who had mercy," was the only neighbor to the Robbed Man.[8] So Jesus told the expert to love his neighbor in the same way the Love Samaritan had loved.

While you may never know how the religion expert responded, you are invited to love your Black Neighbors in the same way as the Love Samaritan. There are a few ways you can respond to Jesus's command, "Go and do likewise."[9] The first two are common yet not what Jesus has for you. The third is uncommon but *exactly* what he has for you.

The first temptation is to say, "This is too hard! Jesus is asking for something that's impossible!" and then to simply decline the invitation. You may not say this aloud, but a part of you will disengage. I get it: Loving your Black Neighbor—or any neighbor—physically, emotionally, psychologically, relationally, financially, and spiritually can feel daunting. I mean, who wants to feel like they've failed before they've even tried? Who likes to be sent on a mission that is in fact impossible? However, if you sulk because you believe the invitation to "go and do likewise" is humanly impossible, then you will remain stuck living in the realm of what's possible through your finite humanity. You will never be able to live in the "all things are possible" realm, which is where the Spirit of Love lives.

You're right if you think that this type of love is hard to demonstrate to one stranger, let alone multiple. If you feel slightly overwhelmed even *thinking* about emulating this kind of love, then I'm right there with you. This type of love can't be copied; it must be grown inside you. It must be birthed by the Spirit of Love. While we may instinctively carry this type of love for those we're tethered to—our children and treasured family and friends—we don't carry it for strangers, particularly those who have been deemed "other." If you want the experience of truly loving your Black Neighbor, then you must acknowledge that you can't love apart from the Spirit of Love.

A second temptation when trying to "go and do likewise" is to try to love your Black Neighbor by yourself, with your own strength. I'm a "to-do list" type of gal, so if you're like me, this may involve crafting a detailed "Loving My Black Neighbor Plan," which could include a list of all the anti-racism books that you will read; following thought leaders and spiritual leaders who write and speak about race, justice, and reconciliation; and maybe even hosting a book club so your friends and family can grow alongside you.

Please hear me when I say reading books about race and racism to grow your understanding is essential. Also, following leaders who can mentor you from afar is beneficial. (One of my favorite mentors is Patricia Raybon, author of *My First White Friend: Con-*

*fessions on Race, Love, and Forgiveness.*) Reading and discussing books alongside listening to trusted leaders can revolutionize both your spiritual life and your worldview.

But I label these things "temptations" because sometimes we conflate external action with spiritual transformation. And too often, we try to love our Black Neighbors with our minds and our strength, when we have yet to learn to love God with our minds and our strength. The temptation is to try to mimic the external actions of the Love Samaritan without experiencing the internal transformation that produces a love that moves our bowels in compassion for our Black Neighbor.

Yet Jesus has a better way for us. His invitation to "do likewise" is, first, an invitation into internal transformation and, second, an invitation into action. The word translated "do" isn't the same as our English verb. Rather, the Greek word *poieō* can mean "to produce, bear, shoot forth."[10] *Poieō* is sometimes translated "bring forth" in Scripture and, in those contexts, generally refers to bearing fruit in our spiritual lives.

In Matthew 3:10, for example, John the Baptist called out the Pharisees (self-righteous religion experts) and the Sadducees (elitist religion experts), saying,

> Now also the axe is laid unto the root of the trees: therefore every tree which bringeth not forth good fruit is hewn down, and cast into the fire.[11]

In this passage, John rebuked the religion experts because they weren't *bringing forth* good fruit. But the rebuke wasn't because they hadn't taken external steps to serve God and their neighbor. As religious leaders, they surely had. The rebuke concerned their *interior* lives, which were reflected externally. We know this because, later in Matthew, Jesus echoed John, saying, "A good tree cannot *bring forth* evil fruit, neither can a corrupt tree *bring forth* good fruit."[12] Jesus went full Oratorical Gangster on them by saying that their lack of good fruit was because their trees were evil.

These religion experts' trees didn't *bring forth* or *bear* fruit from God, which means their seeds didn't originate from God. And because their seeds didn't originate from the Spirit of Love, all their fruit was tainted. In both these passages and in the Good Samaritan passage, this much is clear: The actions we *bring forth* simply reflect our trees. If we bring forth the same kind of fruit as the Love Samaritan did, then our trees are planted, rooted, and watered by the Spirit of Love because "love is of God; and everyone who loves is born of God and knows God."[13] When we bear good fruit, it's a testimony to the Spirit of Love in our hearts. On the flip side, if we don't "do likewise," it's either because we don't want to or because we literally can't since our fruit didn't originate from Love.

Jesus wants us to grasp that love isn't an external action. Love is an interior state of being that is reflected through external action.

So Jesus was saying, "Go and do [bring forth, shoot forth, bear fruit] likewise." He was inviting the religion expert into an internal cultivation process that would lead to fruit. He's inviting you and me into an interior cultivation process that will lead to fruit grown from divine roots.

Throughout our nation's history, so many people have turned their backs on our Black Neighbor. They've pretended they didn't notice the robbery, the brutality, the nakedness, the abandonment, and the need for someone—or many someones—to show love. Some of us have walked to the other side of the road so we didn't have to confront suffering and pain, refusing to allow it to become *our* suffering and pain.

As a nation, we've lost so much by circumventing our Black Neighbor and his needs. We've lost the opportunity for a deeper connection with the Spirit of Love, who can cleanse fear, selfishness, hopelessness, and every type of death that festers inside us. We've lost the opportunity to experience love shooting forth from our hearts. We've lost the opportunity to adorn our country with a glorious crown made of a tightly woven three-strand braid: us, God, and our Black Neighbor.

Yet Jesus's call to "go and do likewise" remains, and he has good gifts for us in the invitation. Jesus has deep internal transformation and compassionate long-suffering for us. He has intimate bonds with our Black Neighbor for us. Above all, he gifts us the Spirit of Love, who guides us as we accept the opportunity to serve our Black Neighbor.

## HEART CHECK

- What would it look like for you to really see your Black Neighbor in your day-to-day life? How might you prioritize your Black Neighbor's acute needs over your time and schedule?

- How do you feel about giving generously and sacrificially to love your Black Neighbor over time? How would it feel to invite others to do this alongside you?

- How is Jesus inviting you to love your Black Neighbor in this moment and beyond?

- What immediate steps can you take to act on Jesus's invitation? Write them down and then do them!

## *Prayer Pause*

*Spirit of Love, I want to love the way the Love Samaritan did, but I need help. Would you reveal any blocks that keep me from seeing and coming close to my Black Neighbor? Give me the desire to love multidimensionally, and help me believe that it's possible through you. Produce divine love in me that will bring forth good fruit. Fruit that will last.*

PART TWO

# Loving Your Black Neighbor

# Love + Wokeness

A few years ago, my friend Michelle, a biracial Black woman, was contemplating the pros and cons of marrying her white boyfriend. She loved him, but she wasn't sure if he could support her well as she navigated racism in America as a Black woman. When she discussed it with some friends, one asked, "Is your boyfriend woke?"

But then a second friend interjected, "That's not the right question. A better question is 'Is he humble?'"

Michelle considered the latter. Her boyfriend was humble, so she married him.

Humility beats wokeness because humility requires love, while wokeness requires only awareness. Humility requires an open heart, while wokeness requires only an open mind. There are plenty of proud woke folks who carry their wokeness like a hammer, trying to pummel their friends and family out of slumber.

You don't need to be woke to love. You need to be humble.

love > wokeness

Yet love *will* awaken us: to our neighbor's needs, to her plight, to her concerns.

To hurt previously unnoticed.

Wokeness ain't wrong, but wokeness must be a means to an end, not the end.

Let's let wokeness awaken us to love.

# CHAPTER 5

# Loving Through Cultural Lenses

In the love of the family of God, we must become color brave, color caring, color honoring, and not color blind. We have to recognize the image of God in one another. We have to love despite, and even because of, our differences.

—Latasha Morrison, *Be the Bridge*

They say you don't really know someone until you've lived with them. Or traveled with them. Or met their family. I say you don't really know someone until you know their love languages *and* their cultural love lenses. Lemme tell you a story.

Once upon a time I loved a man named Anon. He was tall, dark, and handsome, quite literally. His six-foot-three frame towered over my five-foot-six one, and his rich Ghanaian skin was five shades darker than mine. One night, months before we started officially dating, Anon was home sick in bed. I dropped off a pot of homemade soup. "You made this for me?" he exclaimed. His eyes were so big and bright you would've thought I'd delivered a pot of gold.

It was then, because of the look of utter joy on his face, that I should have recognized his love language: acts of service. But this was long before I read Dr. Gary Chapman's book *The 5 Love Languages,* where he explained how couples receive and give love through gifts, physical touch, quality time, acts of service, or words of affirmation. So I only observed that Anon really appreciated the homemade soup.

Once we started dating, I realized two important things about this former Division I basketball player (who still possessed the appetite of a Division I basketball player). First, he didn't really cook. Second, he took groceries to his mom's house every weekend so she could prepare his meals for the upcoming week. I found this practice odd but attributed it to motherly love and the fact that he worked a full-time job and was earning another degree.

When I saw how much Anon loved Ghanaian food and that it was his comfort food, I asked his mother to teach me how to make a few of his favorite dishes. Me, being the modern American woman I am, invited him to learn alongside me—cuz I refused to be the only one in the relationship who knew how to make jollof rice. And him, being the crazy-in-love man he was, bragged to his mom about how good my jollof rice was, even though it clearly didn't measure up to hers.

As our relationship deepened, I told him I'd take over preparing his meals—at least until he completed school. I could help him out *and* prepare my own meals at the same time. But in the back of my mind, I remembered the advice my dear friend Ebony's mom gave her: "Never do anything at the start of a relationship that you aren't willing to do for the rest of your life."

Although our newly minted love had propelled me to make this man's food on the regular, I knew I didn't want to cook all his meals permanently, neither as his girlfriend nor as his wife. So when he graduated from school, my meal service ended. He didn't complain, though. He simply resumed having his mama cook his meals, while I rolled my eyes in silent protest.

At the time, I didn't understand that cooking food was how Ghanaian women showed love to their men: wives for their husbands and mothers for their children. I didn't understand that it was a rich cultural practice, even if I considered it an imbalanced gendered practice. I didn't fully appreciate that it was how his mom had shown love to him all his life and that it was how he was used to receiving love. It was a cultural love lens—a way his Ghanaian heart received love. Also, I didn't grasp that acts of service was Anon's personal love language, even outside his culture. Looking back, I realize that completely stopping the meal service must have hurt him. Our relationship might have been different if I had understood his individual love language and his cultural love lens.

Since Dr. Chapman introduced the 5 Love Languages more than thirty years ago, their use has expanded into non-romantic relationships between friends, co-workers, and family members. The book has provided categories for people of all walks of life to understand how to tangibly express love in different ways. Throughout the last decade, I've used the 5 Love Languages in my personal relationships. In fact, some of my Asian American friends insist that Dr. Chapman missed the sixth love language: food. They argue that in many Asian American cultures, making food isn't just an act of service. It's its own distinctive love language.

After considering their observations and thinking about my experience with Anon, I started to wonder, *If individuals like to receive and give love in specific ways, then could the same be true for cultural and racial groups? Culturally, do African Americans have specific lenses through which they see and thus experience love? If so, what are they? And which shared cultural values have shaped those lenses?* As I dug into these questions, the concept of cultural love lenses and the Black Love Lenses emerged.

In its essence, love is universal and acultural, yet the articulation of love is often steeped in culture. Cultural love lenses are how members of a particular culture show love to one another, and these cultural love lenses are often the primary way they experience love from people of other cultural groups. Culture can develop because of geography, nationality, ethnicity, or purely shared interests, and cultural love lenses situate a person within their cultural context.

Cultural love lenses provide more data points about a person, more dots to connect that will give us a better picture of who they are and how best to treat them. When students write book reports in school, don't teachers always encourage them to research the author's personal history and historical context to gain deeper insight into the book's meaning? You can apply the same principle to cultural love lenses. Understanding someone's culture and its love lenses gives you insight into how to love them as an individual *and* as a member of that particular cultural group. Plus, it brings awareness of how their cultural love lenses interact with and maybe even contrast with yours.

But too often, especially in a multicultural and multiracial society like the U.S., we miss people's cultural love lenses. We miss the beauty of our neighbor's culture—its history, values, and customs—and the many ways they love God. We also miss the tender places of our neighbor's story and risk unnecessarily injuring them.

Some of us don't recognize cultural love lenses because we assume we're all the same. We assume we all have the same values, the same communication styles, and the same lenses through which we see the world. Maybe you've been taught to be color blind, and because of it, you're unaware of the kaleidoscope of cultural differences between you and your neighbors.

When we don't see our neighbors through their cultural love lenses, we can unconsciously and mistakenly believe that our culture's way of doing something is the most loving way. In fact, we may not think to question if there's another way. And if your Black Neighbor is literally your neighbor? Then assuming sameness with your neighbor or believing harmful stereotypes that silo you from them can become easier. When I assumed sameness with my Zambian Neighbor, I mistakenly believed my way of being a good neighbor was the most loving way. Because I loved with the wrong lens, my love didn't reach my neighbor.

The Mubanga family traveled from Lusaka, Zambia, to Pasadena, California, to study at Fuller Seminary. When they arrived at my multiracial church, our church members knew the Mubangas would encounter cultural differences and specific needs because of their status as international students. Did they have a computer for school? A car to get around? Were they warm enough in a climate that, although considered warm by U.S. standards, dipped well below average temperatures in their home country? In big and small ways, our church community rushed to be good neighbors to this family that had flown halfway around the world and now worshipped with us.

Although our church family had the foresight to prepare for some cultural differences, other cultural differences remained invisible to us. In a phone conversation Mary and I had, she told me how these differences had affected her. Specifically, she spoke about the isolation and loneliness she experienced when she moved to the U.S., primarily because she shifted from a communal culture to an individualistic one: "I would've loved it if anybody just came and knocked on my door, other than having to ask, 'Can I come over? Are you available on this date?'"

Mary wasn't accustomed to scheduling appointments with friends.

In Zambian culture, your friends and family drop by unannounced. In her early days in the U.S., Mary longed for her friends and folks from church to drop by just to check up on her.

I had no idea this was her cultural love lens. I never dropped by her house unannounced. I always made an appointment because I thought that was the best thing for her and her growing family. I assumed that she viewed time, scheduling, and visits from her neighbors the same way I did. But in the end, she felt isolated because she didn't experience love in the way she needed to receive it, and my love was lost in translation.

Beloved, when we unintentionally assume our culture's way is the standard, we miss spotting cultural love lenses. When we assume that our values, communication styles, and lenses are better than others'—either subconsciously or consciously—everyone loses. Our Black Neighbor doesn't receive the love she wants and needs, and we miss out on learning new ways to love.

To illustrate, let's go back to math lessons in primary school. Imagine trying to get to the number 4 and knowing only this equation: $2 + 2 = 4$. That's great! But then you realize you can also get to 4 by adding 1 and 3. That's great as well. Next you learn multiplication and see that $2 \times 2 = 4$. You smile because your young mind is starting to understand that math is multidimensional. Over the years you find out that there are myriad ways to get to 4: division, exponents, and more. Your. mind. is. blown!

Cultural love lenses teach you multiple ways to get to 4. When you embrace these love lenses, you learn new ways to show love and you avoid insisting your culture's love lenses are the standard. Lemme put it another way: Embracing other people's cultural love lenses keeps you from insisting your culture's love lenses are superior. To think that the first way you learned to get to 4—$2 + 2$—is the only way is childish. My friend Lily Sue put it well when she told me, "Differences are on purpose. They are a challenge to the quality of our love and to the depth of our obedience to God."

Our differences—be they racial or cultural—challenge us to push past pride and to love in a way that overrides our comfort. These differences require us to press through any obstacles that would prevent us from living like the Love Samaritan. The cost of ignoring the full person—the individual and the culture—is detrimental for you *and* your Black Neighbor: Love isn't given and love isn't received. It's a lose-lose scenario. But Jesus calls us into a full love for our Black Neighbor that overflows into action.

## Love in Action

Imagine, for a moment, that a family realizes their youngest child is deaf. While the child is still a babe, they decide to learn American Sign Language (ASL). Imagine this family teaching their child ASL. See them enrolling this child in a school where other kids speak ASL. See them also able and willing to help their child develop their speaking and listening skills. Imagine this family saying, "We will adapt. We will learn to speak your language, even though it's completely new to us. Even though we're already fluent and comfortable in a different language that's dominant in the broader culture. We will do all this because we love you."

I saw this kind of love in action when my dear friend Kristal, a Black woman, met and fell in love with a man born and raised in France. Although he was fluent in English and had lived in the U.S. for several years, she saw how much his brain tired while working to communicate in English all day: at work, with friends, and when he spoke with her. She saw how much his mind could rest—and how much his personality could shine—when he spoke his native tongue with his family. "That's when I knew I was gonna have to learn French," she told me, months before they got engaged. And she has. She has taken classes. Practiced with him and flown to Paris to practice with his friends and family.

Learning the love lenses of a culture other than your own is a lot like learning a new language. But love will make you gladly learn a new language, even if it's difficult and makes you feel like a little kid learning to speak. Love makes you willingly bend toward another. *Oui?*

Today I invite you to bend toward your Black Neighbor and embrace their cultural love lenses. Throughout these pages, we will talk about some of the shared cultural mores of African Americans, which have been demonstrated and strengthened as we have lived on American soil. I refer to the cultural love lenses of African Americans as the Black Love Lenses. It is through these Black Love Lenses that I ask you to see and love your Black Neighbor. Although these lenses aren't exclusive to Black people in the U.S., I believe they hold heightened significance given our specific shared experiences from African to North American soil.

Please note, I present the Black Love Lenses with humility. I believe the lenses offer insight into the dynamic, always flossin', always glossin' ethnic group I have been blessed to study, write about, and be neighbors with throughout my life. This list of lenses is more insightful than authoritative and not necessarily comprehensive. Some would make the case for including others like the sanctity of life, hospitality, soul food, and music.

I must also note that while these love lenses will help you love your individual Black Neighbor, the Black Love Lenses are as much for the Black community as a whole, because, in addition to being "an uppercase people," we are a communal people who are as tight as the 4-c coils at the nape of necks.

As I sought to identify these lenses, first I thought about our shared cultural values like respect and community. Then I looked at how these values are expressed. I saw these demonstrations of love, these cultural love lenses, all over: in history books, in the news, on historically Black college and university (HBCU) campuses, in my life, and in the lives of family and friends. I even saw them on the pages of Scripture. To give you a better sense of this process, I put together a chart that outlines the cultural values and the correlating Black Love Lens.*

| Cultural Values in African American Communities | Black Love Lenses to Support Those Values |
|---|---|
| Community<br><br>Identifying with the Black community, not solely as an individual<br><br>Always looking out for the community<br><br>Finding ways to give back to the community | Intimacy |

* Cultural values can vary slightly from generation to generation. The values listed here might represent more traditionally held values. Also, some generations—particularly younger generations—might replace "God and Faith" with "Spirituality." Regardless of any shifts or nuances, the opportunity to love cross-culturally through the Black Love Lenses remains.

| Cultural Values in African American Communities | Black Love Lenses to Support Those Values |
| --- | --- |
| Respect<br><br>Being shown dignity and respect<br><br>Being seen and valued<br><br>Respecting others, especially elders | Honor |
| Speaking the Truth<br><br>Speaking up for yourself<br><br>Speaking up about injustice and what's right and true<br><br>Examples: preachers, abolitionists, politicians | Stand Up |
| Standing Up<br><br>Standing up for the truth<br><br>Standing up for your Black Neighbor<br><br>Standing up for justice | Stand Up |

| Cultural Values in African American Communities | Black Love Lenses to Support Those Values |
|---|---|
| Giving<br><br>Giving when there's a need, even if you have to give sacrificially<br><br>Giving to strengthen the community, church, and family | God's-Gifts |
| God and Faith<br><br>Having faith in God's love, provision, and protection<br><br>Praying for justice and righteousness<br><br>Praying for our families and communities | The Spirit of Love |

We'll review each of these love lenses in detail throughout the next several chapters, but I want to offer a brief introduction now. The first Black Love Lens, *intimacy,* welcomes you into physical, emotional, and spiritual closeness with your Black Neighbor. The second Black Love Lens, *honor,* invites you to respect and even revere your Black Neighbor the way God does. The third Black Love Lens, *stand up,* asks you to use your voice and courageous faith to stand up for your Black Neighbor. The fourth Black Love Lens, *God's-gifts,* encourages you to use your resources to partner with God by giving to your Black Neighbor. The fifth and final Black Love Lens is *the Spirit of Love,* the love lens that empowers the others yet is its own category.

## A Posture of the Heart

Around 2001, I had a vision. It didn't feel like a spiritual vision per se but was rather an idea that popped into my head in image form. In this vision, I saw myself taking an all-Black group of college students to the continent of Africa to serve in some capacity. I didn't know where we might go or how we might show love, but I knew I needed to do it. It felt like the homeland I had never known was inviting me back, but for the first time. I felt that she held gifts for me there.

Five years later, I took a mostly Black team of college students to the motherland. Before our feet touched the soil in Kumasi, Ghana, our leaders trained us on local and national customs to prepare us for the cultural differences we would encounter. We learned how to address elders, how to welcome people in Twi—"Akwaaba!"—and to never shake anyone's hand with our left hand because that was considered dirty. The students and I read about Ghanaian culture for weeks before we served at a local school on our four-week trip; we wanted to ensure that we were loving, culturally aware, non-offensive guests.

In both instances—when I traveled to Ghana and when Zambia traveled to me through the Mubanga family—cultural differences were not only assumed but also provided for. The students and I took the posture of learners who wanted to show only love and kindness to our neighbors. By learning our neighbors' cultural love lenses, we chose to communicate at a heart level. We said, *I see you and I value you.*

The Spirit of Love invites you to have the same posture toward your Black Neighbor, whether she hails from a different country, continent, or cubicle. This posture assumes that, despite your best efforts to love cross-culturally, there's much to learn. As you choose to love through new lenses, your heart is willing to bend toward another. Embracing the Black Love Lenses is essentially telling your Black Neighbor, *I know there are differences, and I want to take the time to learn how to love you the way you see love. You are worth bending toward.*

## HEART CHECK

- What are your culture's values and their corresponding cultural love lenses?

- Do you ever think your culture's values, communication styles, and lenses are superior? Why or why not?

- What, if anything, makes it difficult for you to see love through a different cultural lens?

- Which, if any, of the values or Black Love Lenses in the box surprised you?

### *Prayer Pause*

*Spirit of Love, I admit that I have much to learn and that I don't know what I don't know. Would you give me a pliable, teachable heart? Would you give me the humility to replace any assumptions with questions? Would you remove any sense of cultural superiority I may have? Would you show me my own cultural lenses and show me how to love my Black Neighbor with new lenses?*

# CHAPTER 6

# The Black Love Lens: Intimacy in Neighborhoods

Intimacy is the most basic of human needs, as critical to human thriving as sunlight is to plants.

Like love, intimacy is hard to define. Yet you know it when you experience it.

Intimacy is found in a hand placed on the small of a back or in a hug with a squeeze attached.

Intimacy lives where secrets are shared.

Intimacy grows grace spaces.

Much was stolen from enslaved Nigerians, Ghanaians, and other Africans as they were forcefully pushed from the shores of their motherland to a land that promised "Life, Liberty and the pursuit of Happiness."[1] Honor and intimacy were snatched. The intimacy of communing with and living on the soil of their ancestors. The intimacy of forging marriages and families that couldn't be ripped apart by slave auctions and enslavers' erratic whims. Snatched, too, was the intimacy of loving and being loved by their non-Black neighbors in their new land. Intimacy wasn't their birthright on this new soil. No, they carried passports stamped with pain.

Today, however, we have the opportunity to experience intimacy with Niger's descendants.

For there to be intimacy, though, there must be proximity: physical, emotional, or spiritual closeness. To love your Black Neighbor, you have to actually be near him. A neighbor is near you, geographically speaking, or a neighbor might be someone whom you've allowed to be close to you on a heart and spiritual level. Jesus invites you into intimacy with your Black Neighbor both in physical proximity and in your spirit and heart. Intimacy is the first Black Love Lens.

In Luke, when the priest and the Levite "passed by on the other side" to avoid the Robbed Man,[2] they purposefully created physical distance so they didn't have to face how his humanity had been wounded and share emotional space with him. The priest and the Levite hid behind cultural, religious, and personal barriers that kept them from loving the Robbed Man. Likewise, cultural, religious, and personal barriers can keep you from experiencing closeness with your Black Neighbor.

Overtly and covertly, U.S. culture has encouraged you to avoid intimacy with your Black Neighbor and to keep your distance in your neighborhood, at school, in public spaces, at your workplace, and even at church. Governmental policies, the church's failures, and individuals' and families' choices have built barriers between you and your Black Neighbor. Yet the Spirit of Love invites you to come close, to recognize where our culture has erected roadblocks, and to take part in tearing them down. While there are a multitude of ways to cultivate intimacy with your Black Neighbor, let's focus on two specific places: our neighborhoods and our churches. Because there's so much to say about each of these places, we'll start with intimacy in our neighborhoods, then move to intimacy in our churches in the next chapter. But before we learn how to intention-ally cultivate intimacy, we must see the barriers.

## Broken Intimacy in Neighborhoods

In the summer of 2017, I walked up the hill to the college prep cen-ter where I taught English. I was enjoying the gorgeous California sun when I saw a thin white man in his forties, approximately five feet ten, heading toward me on the sidewalk. I paid him no mind as he stepped off the path and into the street. But as he passed by, I heard him mumble, "What are you doing here?" His tone, and the fact that he created physical distance between us by walking into the street, clearly communicated his message: *What are you—a Black woman—doing in this affluent neighborhood?*

I was stunned. My feet kept walking, but my mind was spinning. *Did I hear what I thought I heard?* The question this man posed, al-though racist, wasn't unfounded. Turns out I was never supposed to be in Rancho Palos Verdes.

In the 1930s, the government-sponsored Home Owners' Loan Corporation (HOLC) produced maps that color-coded neighbor-hoods throughout Los Angeles and other U.S. cities. The "best" neighborhoods were green, while less desirable but "still desirable" communities were blue. "Definitely declining" neighborhoods were yellow, and "hazardous" communities were red and to be avoided at all costs.[3]

HOLC was a part of President Franklin D. Roosevelt's New Deal, designed to prevent foreclosures and make it easier for Amer-icans to buy homes. But the color-mapping designations, which led to discriminatory practices known as redlining, were steeped in racism and xenophobia. The presence of African Americans, Indigenous people, Mexican Americans, and other immigrants—

including those from Asia and eastern Europe—had a negative impact on a neighborhood's ranking. Rancho Palos Verdes was a green-zoned city located thirty miles south of Los Angeles, and its HOLC description read,

> Restrict ownership to the Caucasian race in perpetuity. . . . The location has great charm and offers a magnificent view of the Pacific Ocean. . . . The area is protected from the adverse influence of area C-161 to the north by virtue of the hill terrain.[4]

The neighborhood I was walking in, where I taught English to a diverse group of students preparing for college, had meant to exclude me in perpetuity—permanently and for all time.* But how? Two words: deed restrictions.

Deed restrictions are contractual rules that govern the sale or use of property. They can be established by a developer or builder, a homeowners' association, or a seller. In Rancho Palos Verdes's case, the deed restrictions mandated that only whites were allowed to purchase property. These specific restrictions were known as "restrictive covenants" or "racial covenants."

---

**restrictive covenant (noun)**—a covenant with a clause that restricts the action of any party to it, especially an agreement among property owners not to sell to members of particular minority groups.[5]

---

The racial covenant in Rancho Palos Verdes had intended to keep me, my Asian American students, and their families from walking

---

* The U.S. Census Bureau estimated that in 2022, only 1.7 percent of Rancho Palos Verdes residents were Black: www.census.gov/quickfacts/ranchopalosverdescity-california.

the streets, shopping, attending school, and making a home in this space. Adding to the injury, the HOLC description called out the alleged benefit of the hilly terrain, saying that it "protected" Rancho Palos Verdes from some of its neighbors—a yellow-zoned Redondo Beach to the north, and further to the north, North Redondo Beach and Hermosa Beach. The description for North Redondo Beach and Hermosa Beach (D-67) read,

> Construction varies from "shack" to standard quality, with little or no attention to architectural design. Maintenance is generally of a low order.

It continued, saying that although some areas "are of better quality than balance of area, but proximity to oil wells precludes a higher grade. The Mexican population will be largely found in the many arroyos which traverse the area. The area as a whole is blighted and is accorded a 'medial red' grade."[6]

Are you shaking your head like I'm shaking mine?

The oil wells were the reason for the red grade (redline) on the map, which kept Mexican American residents in an environmentally dangerous area and white residents out. The restrictions were designed to block intimacy between white neighbors and their Latino/a Neighbors and Black Neighbors.

When you look at the racial makeup of many U.S. cities today, the effects of redlining are clear: "White Americans still live in mostly white neighborhoods,"[7] while "74 percent of the neighborhoods that were redlined in the 1930s are low-to-moderate income neighborhoods today, and 64 percent are also majority minority neighborhoods."[8] Racist policies designed nearly one hundred years ago kept Black families out of white neighborhoods, stifled the purchase of real estate by Black families, and maintained distance between neighbors.

Take a moment to research the area where you live and/or the neighborhood where you grew up. To see if there's a map for your city, search "Mapping Inequality: Redlining in New Deal America" online.[9] The map is provided through the University of Richmond's Digital Scholarship Lab.

Were restrictive covenants in place? If so, how has that affected who lives in these neighborhoods today?

But let's be clear: Restrictive covenants required willing partners. The covenants were supported *and* perpetuated by the Federal Housing Administration (FHA), HOLC, the mortgage industry, and individual home buyers. For example, the FHA's *Underwriting Manual* said, "If a neighborhood is to retain stability, it is necessary that properties shall continue to be occupied by the same social and racial classes. A change in social or racial occupancy generally contributes to instability and a decline in values."[10] The system was designed to keep white Americans in neighborhoods with posh views, no environmental hazards, and no people of color.

Besides maintaining racial segregation in neighborhoods, restrictive covenants severely limited access to capital for aspiring Black homeowners, creating financial inequity. Neighborhoods labeled "best" received the best loans, while "hazardous" communities were denied loans backed by the FHA. In "The Case for Reparations," Ta-Nehisi Coates wrote, "Black people were viewed as a contagion. Redlining went beyond FHA-backed loans and spread to the entire mortgage industry, which was already rife with racism, excluding black people from most legitimate means of obtaining a mortgage."[11]

In turn, they had to seek out other lenders, which sometimes were predatory. Additionally, the inequity Black families experienced in obtaining home loans limited their ability to build and pass on generational wealth through homeownership.

## THE BLACK TAX

In 2016, Paul Austin and his wife, Tenisha Tate Austin, purchased a home outside San Francisco. They bought it off-market from another Black couple who wanted to help the Austins' home-ownership dream become reality. After the Austins had major renovations done on their 1960s home, they had an appraiser come in. The appraiser valued the home at "$989,000, or just $100,000 more than what the Austins got it appraised for prior to their renovations, despite $400,000 in costs," according to ABC7 News.[12] Convinced that race was a contributing factor for the low appraisal, the Austins conducted an experiment.

They asked their friend, a white woman, to pose as the owner of their home on the day a second appraiser was supposed to come. The woman swapped out the photos of the Black family for photos of her own family. Can you guess what happened?

The second appraisal was for $1,482,000, nearly $500,000 more than the original appraisal amount from just weeks before. Ms. Tate Austin told ABC7 News, "There are implications to our ability to create generational wealth or passing things on if our houses appraise for 50% less than its value."[13] She's right. There's a significant financial cost to our Black Neighbors when they are viewed with tainted lenses. There's a cost when they are asked to pay a "Black tax" just for being Black. Even though redlining is no longer legal, this is one way racism permeates the housing industry. But it's far from the only way.

While the federal government and the housing industry bear part of the blame, white homeowners actively participated as well. Not only did they benefit from the system; they also actively maintained it. They saw no problem with living in all-white neighborhoods. Many liked the exclusivity of it. Regardless, they all signed the racial covenants written into their deeds. It was part and parcel of living in those neighborhoods. Each white homeowner supported these restrictions by agreeing not to sell their home to a non-white person.

Perhaps money was a factor in their decision to sign on the dotted line. The homeowners wanted the economic benefits these covenants provided: better rates, higher property values. They were unwilling to take any hits, either social or economic, for anyone. Or perhaps some white homeowners were bound by pride, believing they and their families were too good to have Black Neighbors. Whatever the reason, they chose to be separate from Black folk.

They could've chosen love, though. They could've chosen to live in neighborhoods with Black people and other people of color, thus weakening the entire system. If white homeowners had sought to curb racism or even valued intimacy with Black folk, they could've gone to court and sued over the constitutionality of enforcing these housing contracts, like J. D. and Ethel Shelley, a Black couple from Saint Louis. In 1948, thanks to their lawsuit, *Shelley v. Kraemer,*[14] the Supreme Court ruled the enforcement of restrictive covenants unconstitutional under the Fourteenth Amendment, which says all Americans should receive equal treatment under the law.[15]

Because the Shelleys chose to *stand up* against the racial covenants, I could walk into a neighborhood that was originally designed to exclude me and sip lattes in a Starbucks with an ocean view. I could stroll down the same sidewalk as the white man who mumbled racist thoughts about me and smile, knowing that I had come into this neighborhood to teach *his* kids.

As a socially conscious instructor, I could actively fight the separation that racism, through redlining, had put between neighbors. My K–12 students, who were all Asian American and white, studied a diversity of stories and writers. I wanted my students to know that diversity holds pots of gold for all. In my classes, we counted the riches of Sarah Rector, dreamed alongside poet Langston Hughes, visited Mango Street with writer Sandra Cisneros, learned all about mulberry trees from author Linda Sue Park, and cut our teeth on the poetry of Countee Cullen. I wanted to give each of my students the sense I had in my all-Black parochial school: Blackness is golden. I built intimacy between my students and their Black Neighbors through the rich voices of Black writers. I brought my students close to their Black Neighbors, if not literally, then definitely literarily.

You can choose a countercultural closeness with your Black Neighbors in your neighborhood and community. Don't miss the opportunity to do what generations before you chose not to do— come close physically, emotionally, and spiritually. Be the loving neighbor that closes the space by cultivating intimacy with your Black Neighbors.

## Cultivating Intimacy with Your Black Neighbors

The small liberal arts college I attended had a population of about 1,200 students. Although I didn't know everyone on campus, most people on campus looked familiar. For the most part, we all recognized one another as neighbors. During the first semester of my junior year, I attended Spelman College, an HBCU in Atlanta, as a domestic exchange student. When I returned to Pomona's campus the following semester, I saw people who I had completely forgotten existed! And not just strangers whom I saw irregularly, but people whom I talked with semi-regularly. Some of these people I considered to be friends. I realized that those people weren't important parts of my life. I didn't have intimate relationships with them. They were kinda like background actors in a movie, people who didn't affect my life's plot in any significant way.

How many intimate friendships do you have with Black people? Are the Black people you know close friends, or are they background actors in your life? Are the Black people whom you interact with at work, at church, or in your neighborhood integral parts of your life? Would you truly miss them if separated from them for months?

Through the media—TV, film,[16] and books[17]—American culture has told you your Black Neighbors are nothing more than extras working in the background to serve the plotline of your life, folks with no significant plotlines worth knowing about.* But as we say in the Black church, "The devil is a lie!" Not only do your Black Neighbors have some dope plotlines in progress; you and your family will also benefit from actively watching and participating in their stories.

But, Beloved, when you don't know someone well, you may find it hard to love them. There's a specificity to loving that's possible only when you know someone intimately. Yes, you can demonstrate love in general ways to your Black Neighbor, and even use the Black Love Lenses with cultural intelligence, but specificity is

---

* The #WeNeedDiverseBooks movement emerged in 2014 because of the dearth of children's books with Black protagonists and other protagonists of color.

queen. Because we all wanna be loved—not just generally and not because we're a part of a specific demographic, but because we're intimately seen as unique human beings. By cultivating intimacy with them, you can love your Black Neighbor in specific ways that communicate they are truly seen and known.

Imma get real honest here: Giving tips on how to cultivate intimacy with your Black Neighbors feels a bit weird and unsettling to me because in many ways it's no different from developing an intimate relationship with any of your other neighbors. However, I will quickly share a few thoughts that might prove helpful.

### 1. Choose to Live in a Diverse Neighborhood That Actually Has More Than One or Two Black Families in It

That's it. That's the whole tip.

If you're saying, "But, Chanté, I can't move right now because XYZ. It's just not doable for me. I want to connect with my Black Neighbors, but there aren't many Black Neighbors in my city! What do I do?"

I hear you. I recognize that you have settled into your neighborhood for various reasons, so moving may not be a viable option. I get it. I moved to the countryside of California's Central Coast to write this book, but the Black population of the nearby city is 0.076 percent! So out of the thirty thousand residents, there are approximately twenty-three Black Neighbors. I mean, I have more cousins than the city has Black residents!

Like me, you may live in a small town or region where there aren't that many Black people, because of the historic impact of redlining or other factors. If that's true, then I don't necessarily recommend that you make it your mission to track down your Black Neighbors in order to befriend them. That could feel a little weird, and besides, you definitely don't want them to feel like they're a project. But when you come across them in town, be a friendly neighbor, and pray that the Spirit of Love gives you the opportunity to develop intimate relationships with some of them.

If you live in an area with only a few Black Neighbors and moving (at some point in time) isn't feasible, then aim to cultivate intimacy in ways that don't start with physical proximity. Virtual groups for any and every interest exist, like writing, gardening, and riding motorcycles. I've met some of my closest friends through my online writing groups. We met online, then met in real life, and now communicate mostly virtually and over the phone. We confide in each other and pray together. There's emotional and spiritual intimacy without physical proximity. Please don't allow the limitations of your physical neighborhood to limit the closeness you can experience with your Black Neighbors.

## 2. Truly Welcome Your Black Neighbors When They Move into Your Neighborhood

On a social media post, my friend Rey, a Black woman, wrote about how she and her husband, Glen, were welcomed to their neighborhood:

> We've lived in our (predominantly white) neighborhood for 4½ years. People pretty much stayed to themselves. Not hostile, but definitely not welcoming. Then, we got a new dog. A husky. All of a sudden, people are waving, smiling, saying hi. One lady even pulled over in her car while we were on our walk for a chat. Several people in the neighborhood know his name. Not ours. The dog's. I'm trying to wrap my mind around this response!

Please don't be like Rey and Glen's neighbors! When new Black Neighbors grace the streets of your neighborhood, walk on over and introduce yourself. Take 'em that "welcome to the neighborhood" gift, whether it's a homemade casserole, freshly fried empanadas, a pot of kimchi jjigae, or a gift card to a restaurant if you know you can't cook. Then learn their names. Break bread together to really get to know one another, and when you see them out walking their dog, yes, say hello and ask about their dog, but also take the time to ask them questions about their lives. Closeness requires connection over time. It's good for you and your Black Neighbors to experience being seen, known, and valued in the spaces you call home.

### 3. Find Where Your Black Neighbors Congregate; Then Go Join Them

Your Black Neighbors likely support the larger Black community by working with organizations committed to racial and educational justice. These groups serve as a source of community for your neighbors and pour back into the Black community through mentorship, college scholarships, and career training. Generally speaking, your Black Neighbors don't live siloed from the larger Black community. They are active participants, often being the hands and feet of Love in those spaces. By cultivating intimacy with your Black Neighbors, you will see love in action and hopefully love alongside them. You will get to see what it's like to take a communal approach to life and love, instead of the rugged individualistic approach American culture preaches.

Not sure where to start? Look in major cities for chapters of the National Association for the Advancement of Colored People (NAACP), the National Urban League, the National Council of

Negro Women (NCNW), the National Black MBA Association, or other organizations committed to racial justice. Some of your Black Neighbors most likely are members of these organizations and participate in their events. So check to see if non-members can attend events. If they can, go to learn; go to serve—not from an elevated place, but instead as the person who sets up tables and chairs, welcomes people to the event, or takes out the trash.

One last note: These are general tips that can be implemented only as relationship grows. Some of these organizations are designed to be safe communal spaces that provide respite for your Black Neighbors from the broader culture. Before you try to serve there, make sure that you have been "invited to the cookout."

### 4. Choose to Get and Stay Emotionally Close

The Love Samaritan chose to get close to the Robbed Man despite and because of the robbery and pain. Being close with your Black Neighbors won't be all doom and gloom, but experiencing intimacy with your Black Neighbors will involve getting up close and personal with the ways the good ole U.S. of A. hasn't loved them. We will talk about this more in future chapters, including specific ways you can get close and stay close.

Remember, when you see cultivating intimacy as your opportunity to serve and your opportunity to learn, then you create the space for intimacy to form. You can't force relationships. Like most good things, they must grow naturally over time.

By loving the Black people in your neighborhood, you can become a part of their community, someone who's both a close friend and a partner in loving the entire Black community.

## BECOMING A SAFE SPACE

The Latina woman slowly stood up before the crowd, walked to the front of the room, and confessed, "I loved the experience this weekend, but honestly, umm . . . this didn't always feel like a safe space."

We were at the final gathering of our weekend-long artists' retreat, and the retreat planners had carefully curated each activity and worked hard to ensure that every type of diversity was represented at the retreat, even among its leadership. I'm sure her critique wasn't what they had hoped to hear. I sympathized with her and contemplated if what she wanted so desperately to feel—what I myself had wanted desperately to feel many times before—was truly possible.

*Safe space* is a buzzword that reflects the need for your Black Neighbor, women, women of color, queer people, and others who sit at various intersections to occupy spaces where they are safe: places where they are seen, valued, not marginalized, and maybe in the majority. But I've come to realize *safe space* is a misnomer because no space is a perfectly safe space.

Although we may rightly long for safe spaces, I believe what we really want—to feel fully seen, known, and valued—is rarely guaranteed within those spaces. Rather, the imperfections of these spaces can reveal how safe we actually are in them.

For example, my family home is a safe space, but sometimes my family injures me. Yet I trust that they will work to heal any injury sustained in that space. And they do. Their willingness to do so confirms that they are safe. They are my safe, imperfect space.

Becoming a safe space isn't about being perfect by never offending someone or never saying or doing something racist. In fact, every callout is an opportunity to grow in racial humility, understanding, and love. Ironically, there's freedom and security when you realize that no space is completely safe for you and that you are never completely safe for anyone. Because every callout becomes a call into a grace space.

In a grace space, you can walk without fear because there is room for mess-ups and cleanups. You can courageously put on new lenses because there is safety both for the offended party and for the offender. You can feel fully free to be called in, and your neighbor can feel fully free to call you out, because a grace space drives defensiveness and fear out. In a grace space, your Black Neighbor trusts you enough to bring up an offense without fear of ruining the relationship. You become the person your Black Neighbor wants to work with through racial conflict. You cultivate real relationships and true intimacy.

So allow yourself to grow into a grace space. Embrace forgiveness for yourself and others, and expect perfection from no one.

## The Gift of Intimacy

In 2021, I temporarily moved from the hustle and bustle of Los Angeles, the city that raised me, to the calming countryside of California's Central Coast. The goal was to write this book while surrounded by nature. What I envisioned were calm, quiet mornings free from speeding cars and noisy horns. What I experienced was a rooster loudly awakening me before six most mornings. What I envisioned was waking up to birds chirping gleefully and me preparing salmon-stuffed omelets with eggs fresh from the chicken coop. What I experienced was waking up to legions of pincher bugs that had decided my cabin was the perfect hideout. My idyllic expectations about living in the country collided with its humbling reality.

But on the flip side, living on the land grew me in so many unexpected ways. My neighbors taught me how to run the generator to power my cabin and how to pump water from the well. They taught me how to garden and that I had to use freshly plucked raspberries within seventy-two hours or they'd go bad—something this city girl who previously bought all her fruit from the market didn't know. My neighbors taught me the beauty of observing the land, of not rushing to the day's demands but being swept away by the sunset's show of amber hues. I learned how to cultivate stillness by simply watching the cattle graze on the rolling hills.

Through physical proximity to and intimacy with my neighbors, I saw firsthand how deeply reliant we are on the land, and vice versa. Moving to a new location with new neighbors changed not only how I see the world but also how I exist in it.

The same can be true for you as you cultivate a close relationship with your Black Neighbor. Yes, at times you will feel a bit uncomfortable—like maybe some pincher bugs snuck into your home. But mostly you will learn the value of things you may not have truly appreciated. More importantly, how you see and exist in the world will change. You will be different—better even—because of your Black Neighbor.

## HEART CHECK

- Do you find a neighborhood less desirable if there are a lot of Black Neighbors? Why or not?

- Do you feel comfortable in environments with lots of Black people? Why or why not?

What is the history of redlining in your current neighborhood or childhood neighborhood?

## Prayer Pause

*Spirit of Love, I don't want to live siloed from my Black Neighbors. Would you help me welcome new Black Neighbors into my neighborhood and help me cultivate intimacy with those I already know? Would you remove every obstacle—real or imagined?*

# CHAPTER 7

# The Black Love Lens:
# Intimacy in the Church

*In flesh-and-blood form, Jesus dwelt among us and was
Love among us—body to body, spirit to spirit.*

Much has been written about the fact that Sunday morning is the most segregated time in America. In fact, Public Religion Research Institute surveyed more than 5,800 adults in 2022 and found that at least 75 percent of white Christians report that their churches are mostly white and that 74 percent of Black Protestants say that their churches are composed of mostly Black congregants.[1] God's house—which is supposed to be a place of love and refuge for people of all nations—became a place of separation.

Yet separation was never the Spirit's vision for us. Intimacy was. How, then, are we to move forward in reversing the separation between neighbors? How do we cultivate intimacy in churches? Before we can figure out the best path toward a collective future, we must identify the path that led us to our present.

The year was 1792, and during this Sunday morning service at St. George's Methodist church in Philadelphia, Minister Richard

Allen did what he did each week: He knelt down to pray. Only this time, Minister Allen, who preached in numerous Methodist churches, was abruptly asked to leave his seat. Turns out Minister Allen and a fellow Black minister, Absalom Jones, had accidentally sat in seats reserved for white parishioners. Minister Allen and Minister Jones didn't realize it until mid-prayer, when white trustees insisted that they move—immediately. To add insult to injury, Minister Jones was physically forced from his knees onto his feet. After the prayer ended, Minister Allen, Minister Jones, and the other Black parishioners left the church, never to return.[2]

Following the incident, Minister Allen co-founded the first Black Protestant denomination, the African Methodist Episcopal (AME) Church, so he and his Black Neighbors could worship freely without the cloud of racism surrounding them. Today, the AME Church has 2.7 million members worldwide, housing more than seven thousand individual congregations.[3] For more than two hundred years, the AME Church has preached the gospel while providing its congregants with a church experience filled with love and free of racism.

As historian Dr. Jemar Tisby wrote in his book *The Color of Compromise,* "There would be no black church without racism in the white church."[4]

While the separation began hundreds of years ago, it has continued in churches throughout the years, including the Assemblies of God (AG) and my Black-led, predominantly Black denomination—the Church of God in Christ (COGIC).

Growing up, I'd known that the COGIC and the Assemblies of God had roots in the Azusa Street Revival, but I'd never understood how the two denominations had emerged side by side, segregated along racial lines: one predominantly Black and the other predominantly white. Did the same Spirit that gave the gift of tongues so all nations could hear the gospel message in their native tongues sanction our separation? The answer was unequivocally no. So I set out to unearth the origins of the separation, which led me back to Azusa Street.

In 1897, a Black minister named Charles Harrison Mason started the Church of God in Christ, a Holiness Pentecostal denomination. C. H. Mason visited Azusa Street in early 1907, where he was touched by the Spirit. He incorporated the COGIC in August of that same year and became bishop of the denomination. COGIC was the first Pentecostal denomination to formally incorporate, meaning that its ordinations were legally recognized and attractive to other Pentecostals who wanted the official recognition and its perks, which included discounted railroad trips.[5] Bishop Mason eagerly built relationships with Black and white ministers alike, who became ordained through the denomination.

Over the ensuing decades, COGIC amassed hundreds of ministers—including many white ministers—all under the COGIC umbrella. Given that the 1910s and 1920s witnessed the proliferation of crushing Jim Crow laws, why did white ministers choose COGIC in the first place? COGIC historian and Bishop David Daniels, PhD, looked to Azusa Street for one possible reason: "Azusa Street captured the imagination of being this church that's not defined by race and that you can fellowship together in this multiracial context and you can be under Black leadership."[6] People were coming to faith, and through all-Black congregations, all-white congregations, multiracial congregations, and Spanish-speaking congregations, the denomination was growing.

Well, kinda. Now, this is the point in the story where historians present different accounts.

There were multiple Pentecostal groups that all went by the name Church of God in Christ. The first group, C. H. Mason's, was the largest. A second group of mostly white ministers also went by the COGIC name from 1911 to 1914. Historians debate whether this group, which disbanded when its leaders helped form the Assemblies of God in 1914, had been organizationally connected to Mason.[7] There were also several white branches of Mason's COGIC, organizationally under his authority, that existed from 1916 through the 1930s. These white ministers and congregations reported to COGIC's general assembly, the denomination's legislative branch.[8]

Assemblies of God scholar Dr. Cecil M. Robeck, Jr., acknowledged, "What now seems quite apparent is that while these white ministers received ordination from the Church of God in Christ, they continued to function along segregated lines. For them, it was a marriage of convenience, not an integrated fellowship."[9] Ultimately, many in this third category of white ministers ended up leaving Bishop Mason and joining the Assemblies of God. By the early 1930s, all-white congregations had completely disappeared from the COGIC.*

The pressing question about their departure is, Why? *Why* did the separation occur?

Did these ministers leave because of theological differences? Did they leave because although they were okay with being credentialed through a Black-led denomination, they didn't really want intimacy with their Black Neighbors? Did they leave because they didn't want to be led by a Black man? Was it a combination of these or something else? In "The Past: Historical Roots of Racial Unity and Division in American Pentecostalism," Dr. Robeck wrote, "To be sure, there were a number of factors which gave rise to the As-

---

* In the 1960s, however, a few white congregations joined the COGIC in California.

semblies of God, but the issue of race was surely one contributing factor."[10]

Dr. Daniels concurred and contemplated the impact of two potential culprits: time and societal pressure. The powerful allure of Azusa Street's culture-shifting multiracial church may have waned over the years, thus dissipating the vision of a unified church. As white ministers became "further and further" removed from the revival, they had to deal with pressing social realities. The racial dynamic prevalent in the 1920s and '30s likely spurred the intentional separation of neighbors in the church. "[Some white] people didn't mind going to a white [COGIC] church, but they had second thoughts if you told them that your supervisors are Black. Because hardly anywhere else in society did whites have Black supervisors." In fact, Dr. Daniels added, "It was against the law in some states."[11] Whatever the specific reason, many white ministers chose to leave Bishop Mason's COGIC and join the Assemblies of God, further widening the gap between them and their Black Neighbors.

While Bishop Mason graciously blessed the creation of the Assemblies of God, separation wasn't what he had envisioned for COGIC. Sadly, the racial unity he had experienced at Azusa Street, where a diverse multitude of God's children worshipped together, shoulder to shoulder, spirit to spirit, didn't grow a racially integrated COGIC denomination.

Instead, the COGIC and the AG have both expanded beyond their roots at Azusa Street to become separate global families of churches. Since 1914, the number of Black members and ministers in the Assemblies of God has grown exponentially. The denomination has repented of its racial sins and welcomed its Black Neighbors. In 2022, 10 percent of the Assemblies of God's nearly three million U.S. adherents were Black, 23 percent were Hispanic, and

56 percent were white; 5 percent described themselves as "Other/ Mixed."[12]

Today COGIC is still Black-led, with 6.5 million members spread across more than one hundred countries including Brazil, Mexico, Canada, and parts of Europe. Approximately two million congregants live in the U.S.[13] Eighty-four percent are Black, 8 percent are Latino/a, 5 percent are white, and 4 percent are mixed race.[14] Dr. Daniels said that in the U.S., from the 1930s until today, "there were and are white clergy who pastor interracial congregations or are members of COGIC congregations."[15]

While the AG has grown to welcome its Black Neighbors, the racial separation that happened with the COGIC and the AG isn't unique. Like the AG, many white churches were formed because of an unwillingness to cultivate intimacy with their Black Neighbors. And like the AME Church, many Black churches emerged as places of refuge.

Dr. Eboni Marshall Turman, theology professor at Yale Divinity School, said that "amidst the Jim Crow South, the Black church was the only place in which African American life and African American identity was affirmed and valued."[16] This was true even outside the South. For me, my COGIC church in Los Angeles was just that: a place of refuge where all things Black were valued and affirmed. I wonder, then, when will white churches become places of refuge for their Black Neighbors? And when will Black churches become places white people want to worship? What will this take?*

In light of the racialized roots of many churches, coming close and staying close ain't in no way easy. Beloved, if we are going to

---

* The racial separation in the American church isn't solely a Black and white issue. I'm focusing on the Black-white divide because it's affected how the church operates cross-racially in general.

close the gap in our churches and cultivate intimacy with our Black Neighbors, then our love must be ongoing and consistent, and it must stand in stark contrast to the lovelessness of the broader culture. For the church to be whole and healthy, particularly when it comes to racial healing, then we must submit to the Spirit and stay submitted to the Spirit, day after day, year after year, decade after decade. Our closeness to one another hinges on our closeness to the cross.

## Coming Closer

On October 14, 2017, Pastor Robert Morris, a white pastor, delivered a message to his congregation about how to fight racial prejudice and love their Black Neighbor. In the message, he described how the Spirit of Love had showed him the state of his heart toward his Black Neighbor by sharing a story that had taken place decades before. His daughter, Elaine, three years old at the time, was playing at their family home with a young Black boy. The young boy's father worked abroad as an athlete and missionary. When the family wasn't overseas, they sometimes stayed with the Morrises.

As Elaine played with the boy, the Spirit of Love spoke to Pastor Morris: "Is it all right with you if Elaine marries a Black man?"

Pastor Morris said, "Well, yes, Lord, it is. If he's a godly man, if he's a man of good character, if he loves her, and if he loves you, yes, it's okay."

The Spirit asked again, "No, is it okay with you?"

When the Spirit asked again, Pastor Morris understood that the question wasn't really a question at all: "I knew when he said that, what he was saying was, 'You still have some prejudices that I need to deal with, but I can't deal with them if I can't reveal them to you. So I need you to be open that you have some prejudices.'"

Then Pastor Morris showed a picture of his daughter, Elaine, all grown up with her Black husband and biracial children.

Pastor Morris continued, "God was already preparing me because what I realized later was that I had things in my heart that I didn't know were in my heart."[17]

On the surface, everything looked great: Pastor Morris, a godly man who taught God's Word to others, was hosting his Black Neighbors who were missionaries. How loving! How giving! But the Spirit saw the clearest picture of his heart. Pastor Morris was willing to let his Black Neighbors come only so close. His closeness to them hinged on his closeness to the Spirit. Would he willingly listen as the Spirit lovingly called out the prejudice in his heart?

When Pastor Morris allowed God to clean out his heart, he received new lenses to love his Black Neighbors. His daughter married a wonderful, godly man. He became a grandparent to beautiful grandchildren who've brought him bundles of joy. His life was enriched because he chose to listen to the Spirit of Love, receive new lenses, and cultivate intimacy with his Black Neighbors.

Like Pastor Morris, when you intentionally draw close to your Black Neighbors, your life and faith will be blessed in multiple ways. You will witness and be challenged to emulate the faithful ways your Black Neighbors love and follow God. Beloved, there are few things more precious than watching your Black Neighbors live out their faith with love and grace in a world that's hell-bent on not loving them.

Imagine what it must have felt like for Minister Richard Allen to be moved from his seat in church that day. For all eyes to be on him as he was told he couldn't freely worship in God's house because he wasn't white. Minister Allen had every right to be angry. He could have let that anger settle into his soul. He could have allowed bitterness to blanket him in self-righteousness. But he clung to the cross, only in an all-Black church.

Imagine how Bishop C. H. Mason felt as he witnessed the racial exodus of white ministers from COGIC. How deep into Love's arms did he have to descend to not walk around carrying bitterness and resentment? I wonder if forgiveness had to cut deep into him.

I'm awed by the extent Black believers must be formed in the Refiner's fire to extend forgiveness over racism day after day, year after year, decade after decade. I'd dare to say they may know the way of the cross in a way you don't yet know.

But you gotta get close to see.

Likewise, I've been amazed at the faith of my Black Neighbors who've traveled to the U.S. from various countries in Africa with zero dollars in their pockets. I've watched them leap across continents with nothing more than a suitcase and a prayer, trusting that Jehovah-Jireh would indeed provide. Amid all of this, I've watched them deal with the crushing impact of colonialism in their homelands *plus* racism in their new land. I've prayed alongside them as they asked God to provide $30,000 over the course of a week, and I've watched that money come in, within *one* week.

These Black Neighbors walk by faith, not by finances, and it has caused me to pray for more faith. Because amid the robbery our Black Neighbors have experienced worldwide, they grasp that faith is faith, which means that the faith you need to believe that God will deliver $30,000 in one week is the same faith you can use to pray that a mountain be moved. Their faith is a beautiful thing to witness, but we can miss it when we don't come close.

When we don't have intimacy with our Black Neighbors at church, we also miss out on experiencing and showing our country

God's power to demolish the racial divide in our land.* We say that with God all things are possible. But are we living in light of this belief? Are we breaking down the dividing wall of racial hostility that has kept us separated since before the U.S.A. became the U.S.A.?

Our witness in our land—our ability to display the resurrection power of Christ—is weakened when our worship is siloed. When we are separated along racial lines, in essence we are telling our culture, *Our God can do anything—well, anything except bring different racial groups together. God can't actually do that.*

The truth is, God can and God will, if we decide we actually want intimacy with our neighbors. That's the starting point. From there, we must take practical steps. Steps that will likely be counter-cultural yet can ultimately be culture-shifting. My prayer is that the church will eventually be a shining example for our nation of how to come and stay close to our Black Neighbors.

## Cultivating Intimacy with Your Black Neighbors at Church

Today I attend a multiracial church, and I'm closer to my church community than I am to many other people. As my spiritual community, they walk with me closely as I work, dream, and make decisions about the future. If you want to be a part of a spiritual community that includes your Black Neighbors, then you must seek to cultivate the closeness you want. There are so many ways to cultivate intimacy, but here are just a few that, honestly, barely scratch the surface.

---

* Some ethnic-specific churches are monoracial because of language barriers. I'm not referring to these churches as I write.

## 1. Choose a Church That Has Black Families

If you want to experience intimacy with your Black Neighbors at church, then you can choose a church that has Black families. Selecting a church in part because of the racial makeup of its congregation may feel a little weird to you, but let's turn to the world of dating to better understand. I'm currently single and ready to mingle! If I want to meet men, then I need to go to where the men are. I can't just chill at my house or at my girlfriends' houses for girls' nights in, thinking I'm gonna meet a man there. If I wanna mingle, then I need to go to the gym, concerts, and sporting events. Likewise, if you wanna mingle with your Black Neighbors at church, then find a church where Black families worship.

## 2. Become Friends with the Black People Who Attend Your Church

Perhaps you've already built community in a specific church, and you feel God asking you to stay. Look for the Black Neighbors in your church, and extend a hand in friendship. Friendships are precious, and they often start with sharing something: a meal, a cup of coffee, a prayer request in a Bible study. So invite your Black Neighbor to dinner or coffee or a Bible study at your home. Build from there, just like you would with any other relationship.

## 3. Make Your Church Hospitable to Your Black Neighbors, Even Before They Step Foot Inside Its Walls

There's nothing better than arriving at someone's house for dinner and seeing that they've already prepared for your arrival. The place is clean, the smell of vanilla-scented candles wafts in the air, and a delicious meal that you can eat is ready because they considered your food restrictions and allergies when cooking.

Similarly, find ways to prepare for the arrival of your Black Neighbors at church. Ask yourself, What kind of music does your church play, either during service or after? Is it all one type, like contemporary Christian music, or is it a diverse selection of music and hymns? On your walls and on your flyers, are there pictures of diverse groups of people, signaling to your Black Neighbors that they're welcome? Also, which Christian leaders are quoted when your pastoral staff preaches? Are they all white? Quoting historic and contemporary Black believers from your pulpit will signal to your Black Neighbors that their presence and perspectives are welcome in your church.

### 4. Mourn Alongside Your Black Neighbors

In 2014, when news channels started reporting more on the unjust killings of our Black Neighbors and people began to talk about the importance of Black Lives, one young white man at my church initiated a prayer meeting for members of our church. Nobody asked him to coordinate this gathering. He did it because his heart was stirred. He was mourning alongside his neighbors, and he wanted to pray alongside us too.

To mourn alongside,[18] you have to understand what your Black Neighbors are actually grieving and allow that grief to pierce your heart. Then you do what you do when someone's mourning: You hold them in prayer by praying for and with them. You tend to their spiritual, physical, emotional, and practical needs.

Often when you mourn alongside someone, you're mourning their loss of a beloved family member or friend. A part of mourning racial injustice is understanding that the mourning is cumulative. Your Black Neighbors are mourning not just a singular death but all the deaths that have come before:

Terence Crutcher

Jeremy McDole

Breonna Taylor

William Chapman II

Walter Scott

Eric Harris

Deborah Danner

Tamir Rice

Akai Gurley

Eric Garner

Sandra Bland

. . . and more.[19]

In light of this, you can tend to your neighbors' practical needs by protesting and petitioning your civic leaders and government representatives until the death, the robbery, and the need for this type of collective mourning end. (We'll talk more about this in chapter 9.)

Mourning alongside your Black Neighbors when they're grieving an injustice committed against someone in their community will show your love and forge intimacy. The deepest closeness emerges not just when you host neighbors for a meal but when you're willing to sit in pain with them.

If you choose to embrace the type of intimacy the Love Samaritan demonstrated, you will see there's a new OTS—an opportunity to sow. You can plant—or sow—intimacy where separation and division have abounded. You can choose to come close when others have chosen to pass by on the other side.

## HEART CHECK

- If you attend church, then how did you select your church? What factors did you consider? Did you consider if any of your Black Neighbors attend?

- Which local churches do a lot of your Black Neighbors attend? Have you ever considered attending? Why or why not?

- If you attend a predominantly or all-white church, then what specific things might you be missing by not worshipping alongside your Black Neighbors?

- More than one of my Black Christian friends have encountered racism as they've dated cross-racially—not from the person they were dating, but from that person's Christian family members. Search your heart. How would you feel if your daughter or son announced their engagement to one of your Black Neighbors? Would you feel excitement or discomfort? If it's discomfort, ask the Spirit of Love to reveal why. Then pray that God removes anything that would keep you from coming closer to your Black Neighbors.

### *Prayer Pause*

Beloved, as you pray today, take time to pause and listen to the Spirit of Love. He longs to guide you and show you how to grow close with your Black Neighbors. As you pray, if you sense or hear something, then take the next step. Make that call. Send that invite. Check out a new church. And if you don't hear anything now, no worries. Eventually the Spirit will instruct you. Let's pray.

*Spirit of Love, open my eyes. Where are you inviting me to experience intimacy with my Black Neighbors? Do you want me to draw near in my neighborhood?*

    \<Pause to listen.>

*Do you want me to draw near at church?*

    \<Pause to listen.>

*Where else are you sending me to cultivate intimacy with my Black Neighbors?*

    \<Pause to listen.>

*God, as I prepare to draw close to my Black Neighbors, give me a clean heart and a listening ear. May I hear your voice as you guide my steps.*

# CHAPTER 8

# The Black Love Lens: Honor

[In the African American community] public humiliation or disrespect is a cardinal sin; it is also an unfortunate fact of life for too many of us. . . . Being the target of disrespect is lodged in our cultural consciousness. . . . When a black person believes he or she has been disrespected, much more is actually at stake than meets the eye for most people. What stands between a disrespected African American and the source of disrespect is almost 400 years of history, four centuries of being the targets of humiliation and abuse.

—Dr. Joy DeGruy,
*Post Traumatic Slave Syndrome*

It's 1995, and my high school U.S. history teacher, a white man named Mr. Z., thinks it will be fun to ask our class where our families emigrated to the U.S. from. My classmates proudly list their countries of origin aloud:

Mexico
Scotland
France

"Here," says Terrance, the only Indigenous student in our class. He and his brother may be the only ones in our entire school. They're half Black, too, and they rep both halves with equal pride. I twitch nervously in my desk as my turn nears. Does Mr. Z. notice my anxiousness? Does he watch my normally gregarious presence shrink before I shyly mutter, "I don't know—somewhere in Africa"? I feel robbed of a connection to a country of origin.

To be completely honest, I feel more than robbery. Embarrassment ensconces me because I am the descendant of enslaved people. While my classmates share heroic tales of their parents, grandparents, and great-grandparents immigrating here for economic advancement, my family lineage boasts no such heroic feats. What's so heroic about surviving? What's so heroic about being the source of someone else's economic advancement, only to be counted as three-fifths of a person? I question my teacher's cultural competency before the term will become a buzzword: *Why didn't Mr. Z. think through the potential consequences of this exercise beforehand?*

Despite the differing details of my classmates' migration histories, their families immigrated here as people; mine arrived as cargo: stolen, broken cargo. Yet somehow I erroneously bear the shame of the crimes committed against them. I don't know that shame isn't mine to shoulder and that the Spirit of Love wants to replace my shame with honor.

Honor isn't a strongly held cultural value in the U.S., yet honor is paramount in many cultures around the globe, from Africa to Asia. In fact, respect and honor are often twin pillars. The 1967 hit song "Respect," performed by the late singer Ms. Aretha Franklin, became a rallying cultural anthem of the civil rights era because it unapologetically demanded that U.S. citizens treat their Black Neighbors with some R-E-S-P-E-C-T.

As a kid, I was taught to respect and honor my parents, the entire Black community, and especially my elders. In our community, respect was something we gave one another—not only because we were made in the image of God but also because, outside our churches, neighborhoods, and cultural institutions, respect was rarely, if ever, given. Respect was how we helped keep others' heads up and spirits high when the forces of racism tried to knock us down low.

Honor is when your cup runs over with respect for another. In Scripture, to honor is "to prize" or "to revere"[1]—to treat someone like they're a prize and to hold them in high regard. Scripture tells us to honor God not just with our words but also with our hearts.[2] We are called to honor specific groups of people, including our parents and widows.[3] And to show the cyclical nature of honor, John 12:26 says that whoever follows Jesus will be honored by God. Honor is how we Black folk have sown love into one another in a country that has repeatedly sown dishonor into us.

The cultivation of honor in the Black community is the thread that stitches together what was ravaged during the transatlantic slave trade and its aftermath. Over the years, as our collective feet have become solidly planted on U.S. soil, the Black community has continuously found ways to honor one another: by treating one another with familial warmth and affection, by affirming one another with a "Well, look at you!" or a "You go, girl!" and by creating our own spaces of honor: the NAACP Image Awards, the BET Awards, the Soul Train Awards, the Stellar Awards, the Carter G. Woodson Book Award, the Coretta Scott King Book Award, Miss Black America, Miss Black USA, and so on. With our warmth, our words, and our awards, we've always found ways to honor the collective we. Honor is our song, our spiritual sinew—binding us together, body to body, spirit to spirit. We've always known that Jesus honors us, too, but who else?

Beloved, when love and respect for your Black Neighbor fill your heart, they will pour out in the form of honor—the second Black Love Lens. And like love, there are as many ways to honor your Black Neighbor as there are languages spoken on Africa's sun-drenched continent.[4]

## Celebrate Your Black Neighbor

The late actress Ms. Cicely Tyson was an iconic TV, film, and the-ater actress who boasted memorable roles in *Roots, A Woman Called Moses, The Autobiography of Miss Jane Pittman,* and *How to Get Away with Murder.* Although her prolific career, which started in the 1950s, garnered almost every award possible, in her memoir, *Just as I Am,* she wrote that as a Black actress she was routinely underpaid for roles. Despite her success, racism and sexism loomed large over her entire seven-decade career.

In 2005, entertainment mogul Oprah Winfrey honored Ms. Tyson by hosting a ball, the Legends Ball, just because. On Insta-gram, Ms. Winfrey wrote, "The idea for the ball originated because I wanted to celebrate HER [Ms. Tyson], and other remarkable Black women who carved a path and built a bridge for me and gen-erations to follow. What a joy to honor her and feel her receive it!"[5]

The three-day ball was a grand display of honor. Ms. Winfrey pulled out all the stops, including a red carpet. Guests attended a luncheon, white-tie event, and gospel brunch that honored twenty-five Black women for their contributions in the fields of art, en-tertainment, and activism. The honorees, which also included Ms. Maya Angelou, Ms. Shirley Caesar, Ms. Aretha Franklin, and Mrs. Coretta Scott King, were celebrated lavishly: I'm talking roses for days, culinary feasts for the eyes and taste buds, and a serenade by none other than R&B crooner Mr. John Legend. The once-in-alifetime event was an elaborate honoring of these Black women as individuals and as a collective. Some might argue that it was too much, an unnecessarily extravagant party thrown by one celebrity for other celebrities, but that's what honor does. Honor goes all out. It goes the extra mile and does the most, because love does the absolute most. Like love, honor knows no bounds.

As I think of the honor Ms. Winfrey bestowed on these Black women, the red carpet she rolled out, I often wonder how it felt to be honored in a Montecito, California, mansion alongside legendary artists and activists. Perhaps it felt like love and honor snuggling up with you, a soft blanket telling you to make yourself at home.

Beloved, you don't have to be a billionaire to honor your Black Neighbors. You can honor them in your home, alongside your community, with the resources available to you.

After college, when I worked with a faith-based organization, I learned that a handful of Nigerian American students had joined our community on campus. I thought it would be great to host a Nigerian culture night where we could learn about and celebrate their culture. Our Nigerian American students brought food, taught us Nigerian worship songs, and wore traditional Nigerian attire. The men sported agbadas, a multipiece outfit consisting of an agbada robe on top with tailored pants and a top underneath. The women wore floor-length dresses made from bright Ankara fabrics and matching head wraps called geles. The event enriched our entire multiethnic fellowship, especially our Nigerian American students, who felt seen, loved, and honored.

During a phone interview more than a decade after the celebration, David, who was a freshman at the time, told me what the event meant to him: "We have a distinct culture with our own clothing and good food. It was cool for other cultures to see, learn about, enjoy, and participate in our distinct heritage. I felt very proud to be Nigerian." The love David and his fellow students felt was palpable. Yet, despite the success of this event, my opportunity to love my Black Neighbors didn't (and couldn't) end there.

## Honor Puts On a New Lens

Several years after the Nigerian culture night celebration, David, who was literally my neighbor (he lived several blocks from me), invited me to his Nigerian church. I enthusiastically said yes. Since I grew up in the COGIC, I know what it's like to be in church for *at least* two hours. Lemme tell you—that Nigerian church service made my COGIC services feel like mini services. Even though it was longer than what I anticipated and what I was used to, even though I wanted to tiptoe out early, I chose to honor him and his church family by fully worshipping until the very end of the service.

Similarly, African weddings and Ghanaian weddings can often be long extravaganzas and may not start at the stated time. I once attended a Nigerian wedding where the ceremony was supposed to start at 11 A.M. but it didn't start until 12 P.M. From my American perspective—time is money—I could have easily become angry and assumed my time had been disrespected. However, I just needed a different lens.

Many cultures in the global majority aren't necessarily driven by clocks; they're driven by different markers and values like relationships or the present task at hand. At the wedding, I experienced a clash of cultural values that forced me to recognize how many cultures have different views on time, communication, and money. My clock-centric outlook on time was not superior, just different. Starting events on time isn't wrong. From my perspective/values, being punctual is a sign of you keeping your word to your guests, honoring punctuality, and recognizing that guests may have other commitments after your event. However, my Nigerian Neighbors had a different lens, with different accompanying values. For them, time isn't as important as the reason we're gathering. And if we have to wait for it to start? No problem—that's more time for the community that's gathered to connect and celebrate.

When I switched glasses, I was challenged to see the relationship between time and community through my Black Neighbors' lens. In that hour or so of waiting, instead of huffing and puffing, upset that I had to wait, I deliberately chose to honor and submit to how my Nigerian Neighbors interacted with time in that moment. I used the time to get to know the people seated right beside me: Who were they? How did they know the bride and the groom? What did they do for a living? What did they do for fun?

When you recognize the ways your cultural love lenses differ from those of your Black Neighbors and choose to embrace a new lens, you choose to cover your Black Neighbors in honor and love. You choose to bend to another. You choose to be like Jesus, who, filled with a deep love and respect for his disciples, bent to wash their feet.

## A Godly Display of Honor

In John 13, Jesus offered one of the greatest demonstrations of honor recorded in the Bible. He washed his disciples' feet.[6] He lowered himself by doing a servant's job so his disciples could receive new lenses and tangibly experience love. To unpack this truth more, let's dig into the full story.

During Jesus's time on earth, they walked everywhere in sandals and on dirty roads. Naturally, dirt, grime, and germs accumulated on their feet after days on the road. When guests entered a home, the servants would typically wash their feet. The layers of dirt, the flecks of animal dung, the dried blood from scrapes—all of it was washed away. The guests never washed their own feet, and the guest of honor certainly never stooped so low.

Yet, on the eve of his death, at the Last Supper, Jesus's final act was not a jaw-dropping miracle but an act of service designed to teach his followers the essence of honor. Jesus had access to everything: power, position, money, victory, life—you name it![7] Then he took all that he had and all that he was, and he knelt to wash people's dirty feet.

Let's pause for a moment to fully grasp this picture. We have Jesus, the revered guest at the meal—a bona fide celebrity of his time. Everyone in the house is watching him, intently listening to everything he says. And at some point during the meal, he gets up, takes off his robe, grabs a towel, grabs a basin, and pours water into that basin. Then—with all eyes on him, all eyes undoubtedly questioning what in the world he's about to do—he bends down and begins to clean feet.

Beloved, God bends to us. I'll say it again: *God bends to us.* God bends to us, in love and honor. God bends to wash our feet. Bends to serve us. Bends to pour oil and wine on our wounds.

We see this lavish love in the person of Jesus. He took the form of a servant, showed us how to honor, and invites us to do the same: to bend to one another, to give honor and preferential treatment to one another—always out of love, never out of obligation.

But when Jesus tried to wash Peter's feet, Peter refused: "You shall never wash my feet!"[8]

Peter didn't understand how Jesus, his teacher and Lord, could lower himself to do servants' work. The social norms and hierarchies of the day dictated that Peter and the other disciples were in no way worthy of having their feet washed by Jesus. But Jesus made it clear that intimacy with him required Peter to allow Jesus to serve him at his point of need: "If I do not wash you, you have no part with Me."[9]

After Jesus had washed their feet, Peter's included, he sat back down and said,

> Do you know what I have done to you? You call Me Teacher and Lord, and you say well, for so I am. If I then, your Lord and Teacher, have washed your feet, you also ought to wash one another's feet. For I have given you an example, that you should do as I have done to you. Most assuredly, I say to you, a servant is not greater than his master; nor is he who is sent greater than he who sent him.[10]

Jesus bent to take care of a practical physical need and to give the disciples new lenses. In contemporary language, I hear him saying, *Look, I'm tryna break down hierarchical thinking here—this sense that anyone is too great to bend down.* Here Jesus was meeting them multidimensionally. Challenging cultural lenses that viewed someone's social position, financial possessions, and family background as determinants of their worth. Lenses that viewed some people as born to serve and others as born to be served.

If we're not careful, we can be like the disciples, questioning who is worthy of honor. Is it the upstanding citizen, the Black kindergarten teacher who greets his students every morning with smiles and daps? Or is it the seventeen-year-old Black man who dropped out of high school, never got his GED, and now panhandles for a living at the corner by your neighborhood gas station? How do we view the never-married twenty-four-year-old Black woman who has three children and has to receive government support because she can't afford to pay exorbitant childcare fees? Do we tell her "You reap what you sow," or do we extend honor in place of judgment and shame?

In the foot-washing story, Jesus lovingly called out his disciples' pride by offering them a new lens, one where honor isn't reserved solely for those who've done everything right. Jesus extended honor to his disciples and confronted the pride in their hearts. He showed the disciples that they had physical, spiritual, and emotional needs Love wanted to tend to. But they had to embrace humility.

Jesus was saying, *If you don't humble yourselves to receive from me at your point of need, be it physical, spiritual, or emotional, then not only will you not be able to receive from me; you won't be able to give from me either.*

When we unashamedly receive the ways Jesus honors us—regardless of how right or wrong we've been—we become able to honor all our Black Neighbors. Honor and multidimensional love can flow into us and our Black Neighbors only when unhindered by pride: The pride of thinking someone's not worthy of honor. The pride of thinking our feet never need to be washed. Or the pride that motivates us to do all the right things for all the wrong reasons.

Let's not misinterpret Jesus's instructions here merely as a spiritual example we should emulate; there are deeper meanings in verses 14 and 15. Yes, Jesus clearly said the disciples "*ought* to wash one another's feet." But the Greek word used here is *opheilō,* which means "ought, owe, be bound, . . . be a debtor."[11] Jesus is telling us that we are indebted to our neighbor and bound to bend and wash their feet.

If Jesus is your teacher and Lord, then you are bound to wash your neighbor's feet. You are bound to honor your Black Neighbor the same way Jesus honors you. Washing their feet isn't an item to be checked off your spiritual to-do list alongside praying, studying the Bible, giving to the poor, and living justly. Washing your Black Neighbor's feet is a natural outpouring because you are *bound* to them and Christ through love.

Think of being bound to someone as having your welfare and well-being tied to theirs. This is commonly the case between parents and children, married couples, and people who have become your chosen family. When you are bound to someone else, intimacy is present. You are responsible for and in partnership with one another. Being bound to your Black Neighbor is connecting your welfare to theirs and taking the time to bend down to serve them multidimensionally. There is no hierarchy, only love.

To keep it 100, sometimes being bound to someone can feel like carrying a weight. Like taking on another person's burdens and injuries in addition to your own. However, the blessings of being bound to another far exceed any burdens. My writing colleague Kim expressed it best when she wrote about her relationship with her son:

> As a parent, I'm bound to my son. I carry the weight of his needs, emotions, and burdens. Because I love him, I am willing to carry those burdens. I am willingly bound to him out of the abundance of my love. Love makes it possible for me to be bound to him. Love sustains me.

I imagine the same is true for you and your loved ones you are bound to. Love sustains you whether the weight of their burdens feels heavy or light. Likewise, the blessing of being sustained by Love while bound to your Black Neighbor is yours, if you'll welcome it.

So I will ask you, Does it feel like a weight to be asked to wash the feet of your Black Neighbor, or does it feel like an honor to be bound to wash? If it feels like a heavy weight, then take a moment to ask the Spirit of Love to remove any heaviness you may feel.

Jesus didn't stop at telling us we are bound to wash. He added another layer of meaning when he said the disciples should do as he had done. That phrase, "should do," is the Greek word *poieō*—the same word Jesus used in the Love Samaritan story when he said, "Go and do likewise."[12] Remember, *poieō* can mean "to produce, bear, shoot forth."[13] It can refer to things that grow, like how seeds grow into fruit. So, when Jesus says you should do as he has done and honor your Black Neighbor, he isn't inviting you to physically wash your Black Neighbor's feet. He is inviting you into a love that *shoots forth* or *bears* this kind of action—a love that is alive, is constantly growing, and gladly bends to serve. To produce this kind of love, though, your heart has to be tilled and cultivated by the Spirit of Love. So Jesus's invitation is first to grow love *through* him and then to give that love *to* your Black Neighbor.

Choosing to honor your Black Neighbor, despite how your culture treats them, allows you to value them through Love's lenses. They receive the honor that many have withheld from them, while you receive clearer lenses. Resultantly, love abounds and the opportunity for intimacy to develop increases. So gladly bend to Jesus's desire for us to respect and honor our Black Neighbors. Every Black Neighbor, unabashedly and lavishly.

## The ABCs of Honoring Your Black Neighbor

Today when I think about my ancestors who arrived on U.S. soil against their God-given wills, I no longer feel shame. I feel honored to come from a lineage of people who survived the unthinkable and were able to maintain faith despite it. Now I see that honor is

God's salve for me and the collective we, our divine wine and oil for generational injury. Honor—the antithesis of shame—is the only appropriate response for those who repeatedly have been robbed and disrespected. I am grateful that, alongside you, I get to honor my ancestors by how we treat our Black Neighbors today.

There are countless ways to show honor, but here are a few simple ways that are worth their weight in gold.

*Adorn Your Black Neighbors' Names with R-E-S-P-E-C-T*
Just a few generations ago, Black men were commonly referred to as "boy." So addressing your Black Neighbor by their name and with a title is significant. By using an honorific with their name, you acknowledge their value and co-sign that respect is their birthright, just as it is yours.

Titles show respect and honor. So when you greet your Black Neighbor who is older than you, use "Mr. Last Name" or "Ms. / Mrs. Last Name." Some folks may prefer "Sir" or "Ma'am." Similarly, when you introduce your Black Neighbor to someone who is younger than they are, it's appropriate to use a title as well. "Meet Ms. Last Name." When at church or events held by the church, "Sister Last Name" or "Brother Last Name" or "Ms. First Name" may be appropriate, unless someone is a leader. In that case, a title like "Elder," "Minister," or "Evangelist" is appropriate, usually followed by their last name. Regardless of the setting, it's always honoring to call doctors by their title, "Dr. Last Name," especially when introducing someone. Try not to assume your Black Neighbor wants you to introduce her by her first name (i.e., "Dalila" instead of "Dr. Dalila Zachary").

Assuming familiarity by addressing someone by their first name can come across as presumptive and thus dishonoring. It can be seen as a sign of you trying to take them down a notch. Remember, these aren't just titles of respect; they're markers of honor. Better to dole out too much honor than not enough.

## *Behold Their Beauty*

While simple, it's vital that you *really* look at your Black Neighbor and behold their God-fashioned beauty. We can honor our Black Neighbor by looking at their face and into their eyes. When you really look at them and take in their face (its moles and dimples), their hair (its straightness or coarseness), their frame (its strength or frailty), then you see them as a unique person and don't just see their skin color. Not only is it a foundational courtesy we should give all our neighbors, but really looking at your Black Neighbor can also prevent racial profiling and its damaging toll.

In October 2022, Bobbi Wilson, a Black girl from Caldwell, New Jersey, was trying to love her neighborhood by protecting it from the spotted lantern fly. Bobbi had heard about the insect that damaged trees and, per encouragement from her state's Department of Agriculture, wanted to do her part to protect her neighborhood. So the nine-year-old student created her own homemade mix to kill the pests, then sprayed trees near her house that seemed infected by the lantern flies.

But that morning, one of her neighbors, a white man (who happened to be a former councilman for their city), called the police on her. He told the police dispatcher he saw a "little Black woman, walking, spraying stuff on the sidewalks and trees."[14]

Y'all, he described a nine-year-old as a "little Black woman." He mistook a little girl for a fully grown woman! *Why?* Because he didn't really look at her. He didn't behold the beauty of his energetic nine-year-old neighbor. Also, he told the dispatcher that he was scared. Scared of a little Black girl. Who held a spray bottle. In broad daylight.

Monique Joseph, Bobbi's mom, said that following the confrontation with the police, her daughter was afraid to go outside.[15] Ms. Joseph was also baffled as to why her neighbor, who had lived across the street from them for eight years, would call the police on her young daughter. I wonder too.[16]

If you're wondering if he's an outlier, consider that decades of scientific studies have shown that cross-racial bias exists when a member of one racial group tries to identify a member of another racial group, leading to many cases of misidentification.[17] When the misidentification happens in legal cases, it leads to false convictions, jail time, and worse. In 2019, *The Washington Post* reported on a study released by the federal government's National Institute of Standards and Technology, which said that facial recognition systems used by law enforcement agencies "misidentified people of color more often than white people," noting that "Asian and African American people were up to 100 times more likely to be misidentified than white men, depending on the particular algorithm and type of search."[18] *Can you believe that?* I'm trying to wrap my mind around the fact that it's common for my non-Black neighbors—*and* their AI creations—not to truly see their Black Neighbors. Beloved, if we don't take the time to actually *see* our Black Neighbors, then we are more likely to disrespect and dishonor them.

There's power in looking someone directly in the eye. Besides suggesting you ain't shady, in Black American culture, when used in combination with a warm smile, looking someone in the eye can show respect.* Looking someone in the eye is how you acknowledge their presence and let them know—if only for a moment—*I*

---

* In other cultures, eye contact can indicate disrespect. When you take the time to learn your neighbor's culture, you learn these distinctions and can honor them in culturally appropriate ways.

*see you.* So when you come across your Black Neighbor—be it at work, church, or the grocery store—take the time to really look at them.

### Connect Your Black Neighbors to Their Community

On Tuesday, July 12, 2016, I slipped into my church's women's small group, emotionally spent. I mourned the deaths of an unarmed Black man named Alton Sterling who was killed by the Baton Rouge police on July 5 and of Philando Castile, another unarmed Black man who was killed by a Minnesota cop the following day. Their deaths felt personal, like two of my blood relatives had been shot, one right after the other. Each bullet that bloodied their bodies had bloodied my heart. My appetite had disappeared, and my ability to focus had vanished.

I didn't have to tell the white women in my small group that I was grieving. They had heard about the shootings in the news, and these women had connected the dots between Mr. Sterling and me, between Mr. Castile and the collective we. They understood that we Black folk are cultural kinfolk, connected by centuries of oppression we've survived because we had one another's backs and prayed against the Evil One. On this evening, these white women held space for me to share, mourned with me, and prayed for me and our nation.

Unbeknownst to many, millions of Black people in the U.S. carry invisible reservoirs of grief. So when you hear about the shooting of your unarmed Black Neighbor, know that your other Black Neighbors are probably carrying extra grief in their reservoirs. Treat them with the same care and tenderness you'd show to anyone in mourning. When you hear about a neighbor threatening to call the police on an eight-year-old Black girl as she sells water outside her San Francisco apartment[19] or hear about a twelve-year-old Black boy in

Ohio having the police called on him as he runs his lawn-mowing service,[20] know that your Black Neighbors are probably carrying extra grief that week. Consider the disrespect and dishonor they have experienced, and then honor them in every way you can.

*Direct Your Black Neighbors to the Front of the Line*

Historically in the U.S., Black people have been told to go last or to go to the back. To go to the back of the bus, the back of the line, the back of the church. Being first has never been our birthright on U.S. soil, regardless of our citizenship status. So what would it look like for you to let your Black Neighbor go first? What would it look like for you to go against the status quo that says they should be last and instead put them first?

What if during a business meeting, instead of stating your opinion first, you asked your Black colleague to share their thoughts first? What if when you were invited to speak at a conference or asked to be interviewed by a reporter, instead of saying yes, you recommended an equally (if not more) qualified Black Neighbor to do it instead?

Gladly showing preferential treatment is one way you can display honor to your Black Neighbor.[21] Letting your Black Neighbor go first—in the checkout line, in the voting line, or in the Starbucks morning rush—can train your heart to honor in larger ways.

As you allow Jesus to wash your feet, you can receive new lenses and more of his love. Like the Love Samaritan, you can sow honor where dishonor has been sown. Alongside the Spirit of Love, you get to wash away some of the dirt and grime that racism has lobbed onto your Black Neighbors' feet. I've presented just a few ways to honor—A, B, C, and D—but there's a whole alphabet left! Get creative, and ask the Spirit of Love to show you other ways to honor your neighbors.

## HEART CHECK

🔎 Do you see any of your Black Neighbors as unworthy of honor? If so, what impact has that lens had on your love?

🔎 How does it feel to consider giving your Black Neighbors preferential treatment? Does it feel inspiring? Challenging? Unfair?

🔎 Does your culture teach you to see people solely as individuals without any connection to their larger ethnic group? If so, how does that affect how you see and honor your Black Neighbors?

### Prayer Pause

*Spirit of Love, may your boundless love overfill my cup and pour into my Black Neighbor. Guide my actions, and give me new lenses so I can see and honor my neighbor. Is there a specific Black Neighbor—an individual or group—that I can show honor to? Tune my ears to hear your voice so I may know how I can show honor to my Black Neighbor.*

# CHAPTER 9

# The Black Love Lens: Stand Up

Stand up. . . . Show love.

—"Stand Up" by Joshua Henry

"What would you do if you were having dinner with your sponsees and one of them said something racist?" asked a residence hall staff member at my college.

"Well, I would obviously say something," I replied. I was being interviewed to become a sponsor at my college. Sponsors were sophomore student leaders chosen by the residence hall staff to provide community and support to first-year students. Each new student was assigned two sponsors and placed into groups that consisted of a dozen or so students.

Turns out the staff liked this answer and my other answers, and I was selected. At the end of my sophomore year, the residence hall staff invited all the current sponsors to help them interview potential sponsors. In the interviews, they were asked the same question I had received the year before: "What would you do if you were having dinner with your sponsees and one of them said something racist?"

I couldn't imagine anyone would answer this question differently than I had. But when my group interviewed some white students, not one of them said they would do anything about the situation. Not one. Instead, each person gave some version of "I wouldn't want to make the situation weird or call anyone out. I wouldn't want to put anyone on the spot or offend anyone."

Now, I'm sure there were other white students and students of color whom I didn't interview that *did* say they would do something, but in the interviews I conducted, I saw firsthand the culture of silence that can prevail when dealing with racism. I saw how seemingly smart, fair, and justice-minded people can shrink back. And I saw how this can create an environment where their Black Neighbor and others aren't loved. I was hurt and disappointed.

If these young adults, these liberal arts students who claimed to be justice-seekers, couldn't call out racism in a casual conversation in a college cafeteria, then how could they call it out in a city council meeting? How could they call it out in a prestigious corporate job where they occupy a cush corner office? If they couldn't be faithful with a little, then how could they be faithful with much?[1] Could they ever receive the reward that comes from standing up for their Black Neighbor, despite the potential costs?

Decades before the institution of slavery would be outlawed in the U.S., a Black woman, Ms. Isabella Baumfree, escaped from slavery. When she ran away from the house where she had been enslaved, she learned about a safe place—the home of a white couple that abhorred slavery—where she could stay. But soon thereafter, Ms. Baumfree's enslaver found her. He demanded that she return, but she refused. Knowing she would run away again if he dragged her back, he offered a compromise: "Well, I shall take the *child*," he said, demanding the child she clutched in her arms.

As Ms. Baumfree faced the choice between her freedom and

the only child she had managed to bring with her, Mr. Isaac Van Wagenen, the man she was staying with, intervened. In *Narrative of Sojourner Truth* by Ms. Sojourner Truth and Mr. Olive Gilbert, the authors wrote that Mr. Van Wagenen "had never been in the practice of buying and selling slaves; he did not believe in slavery; but, rather than have Isabella taken back by force, he would buy her services."[2]

Before Isabella's enslaver left, Mr. Van Wagenen asked her not to call him master, saying, "There is but *one* master; and he who is *your* master is *my* master."[3] Mr. Van Wagenen wanted Isabella and her former enslaver to know that the only master anyone should be subject to was God, the one who saved people from chains instead of binding them with chains. Mr. Van Wagenen was declaring that he and Isabella were equals; his statement lovingly and forcefully weakened the oppressive chains of slavery in Isabella's and her child's lives. Isabella believed that he and his wife were "undoubtedly a portion of God's nobility."[4] Mr. Van Wagenen's decision to tell the truth, shame the devil, and stand up for Isabella planted the seeds that would enable Isabella to stand up for her Black Neighbor in ensuing years.

I don't know everything that Mr. Van Wagenen risked by standing up for Isabella. I'm not sure if he risked economic loss, being taken to court, or being shunned socially, but he refused to be silent about a system that brutalized Black bodies and souls. In addition to refusing to be silent about it, he used his resources to love his Black Neighbor. If Mr. Van Wagenen were alive today, I believe he'd have no part in the culture of silence around racism that's so prevalent in the world. Not only would he have something to say, but he'd also then go out and do something.

In the book *Then They Came for Mine: Healing from the Trauma of Racial Violence,* Tracey Michae'l Lewis-Giggetts wrote about the

impact of our white neighbors remaining silent about the many in-
justices against our Black Neighbors:

> I can't help but consider the impact of silence on the collective of
> Black folks. I can see how, above and beyond the actual events of
> racial violence—say, the eight minutes and forty-six seconds that
> Derek Chauvin held his knee on George Floyd's neck, the nu-
> merous not-guilty verdicts—what aggravates many Black peo-
> ple is the fact that those injustices are followed by a stark silence,
> particularly from the church. It feels like white Christians be-
> lieve that if we don't talk about race—the "r-word"—then they
> don't have to confront it. The pain that racial violence causes
> goes unseen and ignored. Too many Black folks are sitting in
> churches, just like I was, waiting for someone to see them, love
> them, stand in solidarity with them. We are sitting there hoping
> that the teachings on "Bear one another's burdens" (Gal. 6:2) and
> "Weep with those who weep" (Rom. 12:15) are true. And some-
> times we are seeking a way rooted in love that will allow the rage
> to not consume us.[5]

Beloved, if you want to follow Jesus, then you are called to bear
your Black Neighbor's burdens. You are invited to hold and carry
these burdens as if they were your own, with tenderness and care.
When your Black Neighbor has been knocked down, choose to
bear the burden by speaking up. *Stand up* to injustice. *Stand up* to
the culture of silence that glosses over the injustice. Jump at the
opportunity to serve through the next Black Love Lens: *Stand up*.

Have you ever participated in the culture of silence? Has there
been a time when standing up for your Black Neighbor felt hard
so you just didn't do it? Perhaps your boss or city council member
set a racist policy in place and you knew that it was wrong but said

nothing? Or your uncle or grandparent made a racist joke and, instead of speaking up, you laughed along? Whatever the situation, compliance with this culture of silence—being unwilling to tell the truth when racism is at play—keeps you from loving your Black Neighbor, keeps you from loving God, and keeps you from loving yourself. By being unwilling to challenge social norms, policies, and structures because they feel either too big or too powerful, you abdicate your power and your love.

In those moments of silence, perhaps you lack the courage to speak up. Perhaps your stomach turns, your knees buckle, and your tongue fails you. When fear takes over, turn your heart toward God. He's got you. He will support you no matter the potential costs of standing up for your Black Neighbor. Like he did for Rahab, a woman in Scripture, God will endow you with courage.

## When Faith Overcomes Fear

Let's meet Ms. Rahab through an imagination exercise.

I want you to really think about her as a person, not as a historical heroine. I want you to imagine a single woman who lived in the land of Canaan (the Middle East) before 1000 B.C. Imagine a woman who most likely sat on the margins of her culture, a woman who wasn't protected by a husband either legally or financially. A woman who learned to take care of herself by any means necessary, including entertaining all kinds of men in her home.

In Joshua 2, the king of Jericho sent Ms. Rahab a message, demanding that she hand over the spies who had come to check out the city in preparation for an invasion. Being a spiritually savvy woman, Ms. Rahab knew that Jericho was part of the land that God had promised to give the Israelites after they left enslavement in Egypt. She recognized, too, that her government was corrupt and that her people, the Canaanites, opposed God. Ms. Rahab under-stood that she and the city's other residents were essentially renters on land they didn't own. She had heard about how powerful the Israelites' God was, and she was determined that when all was said and done, she and her family would be left standing. So Rahab lied to the king and said that the two spies had come and gone, even though she was hiding them in her home.

Although Ms. Rahab *technically* lied, her words aligned her with the Truth. In verse 11, she told the spies, "The LORD your God is God in heaven above and on the earth below." Essentially, she said, "I'm not gonna support my king and culture just because that's what I've been told to do. I'm gonna *stand up* for your God, the True King." Ms. Rahab wasn't deemed a "stand up" person (she was a prostitute), but she risked her life to stand up against the king on behalf of the Israelites and their God.

Throughout the story, Ms. Rahab showed so much love to the spies. Because she honored their God, she honored them. She showed them the same level of love and protection you'd show a family member or close friend: She hid them in her home and lied to protect them, even though it meant risking her life. She also experi-enced intimacy with them—and I ain't talkin' about her profession! Ms. Rahab was willing to be associated with and in physical proxim-ity to men who were feared and hated in her land, something most people would never do. She fed them, gave them water, and served them emotional support. (I mean, how would you feel if you were a spy in another country and Wanted posters of you were circulating around town because the king had put out a hit on you?)

Ms. Rahab's *stand up* saved the spies' lives and lineage. Right be-fore the spies left her house, she pulled them aside and said, "Look, I know what's about to go down when y'all return. Please protect my family when it all goes down." They said yes to her request.

There's much we can learn from Ms. Rahab about how faith in God can translate into love for our Black Neighbor. The heart of Ms. Rahab's actions wasn't courage. It was faith. Ms. Rahab is canonized in Scripture because of the faith she had in God, demonstrated through her treatment of these two visitors: "By faith the harlot Rahab did not perish with those who did not believe, when she had received the spies with peace."[6]

In this verse, *faith* has two meanings: "the conviction that God exists and is the creator and ruler of all things" and "fidelity, faithfulness."[7] The first component of faith is a belief in God, while the second is a commitment to God. So faith is belief *plus* action: a belief in God *and* a faithfulness to God through our actions. This idea is echoed throughout Hebrews 11 as the author praised our faith ancestors (aka "the ancients") for the actions they took.[*]

The same faith Ms. Rahab and our other ancestors demonstrated is available to you. Your faith in God gives you the courage to *stand up* for your Black Neighbor. But you have to *step out* on faith and act. In other words, you have to *stand up* in faith!

Because of faith, Ms. Rahab trusted more in the power of God to protect her than in the power of the king to punish her. Because of faith, she believed that God's kingdom would rule over all opposing kingdoms. Because of faith, she chose allegiance to God over allegiance to her king, city, and culture. As a result, she and her family literally got to usher in the kingdom of God as part of Jesus's lineage.[†]

Through Ms. Rahab's story, we clearly see she wasn't ruled by fear. Was she scared? Most likely! I mean, imagine receiving a mes-

---

[*] Please read Hebrews 11. Reading it will help you better understand the enduring power of faith and how it connects with loving your Black Neighbor.
[†] Old Testament passages prophesied that Jesus would be a descendant of King David; Ms. Rahab was the great-great-grandmother of David.

sage from the king, refusing to do as he asked, and *not* being afraid. But our faith can overcome fear.

Ms. Rahab chose to *stand up* to a king and his crew, alone. Like her, we too can *stand up* to an unjust nation, a corrupt city, or unfair school policies that rob our Black Neighbor. Like Ms. Rahab, through faith we can trust that God's power is greater than the power of any potential retaliation.

As you *stand up* in faith, as your courage blooms, I wonder which stories you and your family will become a part of? Which unwritten stories is the Spirit of Love inviting you to partner in? Will you play a part in removing racist clauses in your neighborhood's housing contracts or removing racist monuments in your city? As you *stand up* in faith, the Spirit of Love offers countless ways to love and protect your Black Neighbor. Here are a few ways I personally felt excited to write about.

## Stand Up for Black Honor

After the American Civil War ended in 1865, more than 1,500 Confederate monuments and symbols emerged across thirty-one states. Most of the approximately seven hundred monuments were erected from the 1890s to the 1950s, during the Jim Crow era, with a spike between 1900 and the 1920s.[8] Enraged white southerners raised many of these monuments to protest their bitter loss and tout the belief that they had the right to enslave their Black Neighbors.

The veneration of Confederate war "heroes" through statues and other memorials was a brutal slap in the face to every Black person and every U.S. citizen who cherished liberty and love for all. Few things are more disrespectful and dishonoring than constantly seeing people who fought for your degradation celebrated publicly, for generation after generation to see.

In the summer of 2015, Ms. Bree Newsome Bass *stood up* for her Black Neighbors by climbing the flagpole on the South Carolina State House grounds to remove South Carolina's Confederate flag.[9] Afterward, she was swiftly escorted to jail. Two short weeks later—after Ms. Newsome Bass's act, after nine Black parishioners were killed in a racially motivated shooting at Emanuel African Methodist Episcopal Church,[10] and after decades of protest—the flag was finally removed.

Five summers later, in 2020, the city of Richmond, Virginia, sought to remove the fourteen Confederate monuments, including the equestrian statue of General Stonewall Jackson,[11] that had towered over the former capital city of the Confederacy for more than a century. However, the city says the white contractors they approached to remove them refused. They feared the social and economic pushback they would experience from their white neighbors as a result. Eventually a Black man, Mr. Devon Henry, who owns Team Henry Enterprises, accepted the job as lead contractor on this project, despite the threats made against him.[12] He was the one willing to *stand up* with his Black Neighbors.

Like Ms. Newsome Bass and Mr. Henry, you too can honor your Black Neighbors by removing the places of dishonor in your area. Are there any monuments, statues, street names, flags, or events that celebrate slavery, the Confederacy, racism, or segregation throughout your city, county, or state?* If so, *stand up* for your Black Neighbors by petitioning and protesting for their removal. You can do this legally or take a more radical approach that lands you in jail, like Ms. Newsome Bass did. Throughout U.S. history, protesters have used legal and illegal means to *stand up* for their neighbors, be-

---

* Your city or region's historical society might point you in the direction of where to locate this information.

cause, unfortunately, every law and system ain't just and the unjust ones won't change until we *stand up*.

## Stand Up for Black History

Did you know that Black History Month originated as Negro History Week so that African Americans could learn about their contributions to U.S. culture because textbooks had omitted many of them? Over time, Black History Month evolved into a time where all Americans could learn about and celebrate the contributions of their Black Neighbors.* However, the historical accuracy of school textbooks is still under scrutiny.

In 2015, Dr. Roni Dean-Burren, a Black mom in Texas, discovered that her son's high school geography book referred to enslaved Africans as "immigrants" and "workers."[13] The textbook's publisher whitewashed and revised the history of slavery by suggesting that enslaved people came to the U.S. willingly as free, paid workers. *Can you believe that?!* Just writing it fills me with rage. Rage because my enslaved ancestors were brutalized through slavery and were now being dishonored through this revisionist retelling of history.

After reading her son's textbook, Dr. Dean-Burren complained about the inaccuracy, and the textbook's publisher changed the wording to reflect the truth. Like this mom, you can *stand up* for your Black Neighbors by making sure that all history books and curriculum tell "the truth, the whole truth, and nothing but the truth."[14] Check out the textbooks and overall curriculum at your local schools. Are they truthful? Does the curriculum reflect the

* Black History Month is also celebrated in other countries around the world.

breadth and depth of your Black Neighbors' contributions to the U.S. and the world?

*Standing up* for accurate representation in schoolbooks, classrooms, and libraries is more important than ever. As of 2023, the battle for truth-filled books rages across the U.S. According to PEN America, a non-profit dedicated to ensuring free expression through literature, from July to December 2022, 874 books were banned from classrooms.[15] The organization also reported that "in this six-month period, 30% of the unique titles banned are books about race, racism, or feature characters of color."[16] Books that honor your Black Neighbors and reflect their lives in the U.S. are being stripped from schools.

But without these powerful representations, how can we hope that our children, their children, and their children's children will respect and love through differences? How can we avoid the sins of the past? How can we see our Black Neighbors with clear lenses that cultivate love when we can't understand the breadth and depth of their experiences, past and present?

Read through the books in the curriculum to see if they honor your Black Neighbors. Are the Black characters the protagonists or supporting characters? Is there a diversity of stories about your Black Neighbors? Stories about young Black women who travel to space and stories about disabled Black boys who become fine artists and museum curators? Are there books from Black authors and illustrators? Do they reflect the experience of your Black Neighbors in America and throughout the African diaspora? Or is something missing that landed on the banned-book list? If so, talk to the staff at your local school: the principal, librarian, and teachers. In some cases, you may need to talk to your school district leaders. Alongside other parents, raise your voice to *stand up* for your Black Neighbors.

If your school needs additional resources, consider donating books by Black authors and consider setting up a free little library in your front yard with books that honor your Black Neighbors. Find a way to stand up for your Black Neighbors by ensuring that the truth of their experiences is included.

Here is a short list of honoring, truth-filled books that have landed on schools' banned-books list:

| | |
|---|---|
| *Between the World and Me* by Ta-Nehisi Coates | A seminal book on being Black in America. |
| *Thank You, Jackie Robinson* by Barbara Cohen | Describes the friendship that emerges between a young white boy and an elderly Black man over a mutual love of the Brooklyn Dodgers. |
| *The Story of Ruby Bridges* by Robert Coles | How a young Black girl came to de-segregate public schools in the U.S. |
| *The Life of Rosa Parks* by Kathleen Connors | How a Black woman's courage started the Montgomery bus boycott. |
| *Last Stop on Market Street* by Matt de la Peña | A beautiful and poetic tale of a Black boy taking a trip to serve his neighbors. |

## BROADEN YOUR NEWS SOURCES

It's more difficult to bear your Black Neighbor's burdens when you don't know what they are. You can strengthen your *stand up* by knowing the issues that deeply affect the Black community.

Black media outlets *EBONY* and *Jet* emerged in 1945 and 1951, respectively, because mainstream publications refused to celebrate the contributions of Black folk and cover the topics that affected the Black community.[17] Today newer publications like Faithfully Magazine, TheGrio, NewsOne, AfroTech, Black Enterprise, and Shadow and Act continue to *stand up* for their Black Neighbors by highlighting the issues that affect us the most.

If you want to learn about more ways to speak up and *stand up,* then read the publications that intentionally honor your Black Neighbor through their coverage.

## Stand Up for Black Hair

Did you know that in 2018, six-year-old Clinton Stanley, Jr., arrived for his first day of school with a wide grin and backpack in tow, only to be sent home because his hairstyle violated the school's dress code?[18] The Christian academy in Florida maintained that this young scholar-in-the-making's ethnic hairstyle, locs, was inappropriate for a learning environment. Unfortunately, his school's discriminatory policy isn't unique. Many other schools, both private and public, have similar dress code policies. Even some corporations have similar policies.

These racist policies are in place because, by and large, American culture doesn't consider natural Black hair and Black hairstyles either beautiful or professional. Our hair is othered. We're often told that if we want to secure a good job or even attend school, then we must conform to white, Eurocentric standards of beauty that prefer long, straight, perfectly manicured hair. Your Black Neighbors are fighting an ongoing battle for the right to wear our hair in ethnic hairstyles like locs, braids, and twists.

In 2019, California became the first state in the nation to ban race-based hair discrimination in workplaces and public schools. Since then, the CROWN Act, which stands for "Creating a Respectful and Open World for Natural Hair,"[19] has been replicated and passed in cities, counties, and states throughout the country—with varying levels of success. Much is at stake:

- Black children growing up seeing the diversity of Black hair represented and celebrated in schools, in boardrooms, and on TV.
- Black people not being denied jobs and promotions because we aren't willing to contort our hair (and by extension ourselves) to fit beauty and dress code standards that dishonor us.
- Black people getting to sashay on the catwalk of life as our authentic, free selves, showing off the beautiful crowns the good Lord gave us!
- All people understanding that, by divine design, Black hair and Black people are beautiful.

*Stand up* for your Black Neighbor by asking about the dress code policies at your job and local schools. Then ask yourself, Are the policies written to include diversity and ethnicity? If not, talk to your boss, your human resources representative, the legal department, the school principal, or the board of education. You can also *stand up* by writing to your political representatives if your city, county, and state haven't passed the CROWN Act.* Then write to your federal representatives because, as of the writing of this book, the act hasn't passed at the federal level.

## Sojourner's Seeds

After Isabella was freed from slavery, she took on a new name, Sojourner Truth. No doubt she felt called—perhaps destined—to journey on a path where she would proclaim how God felt about her and her Black Neighbors: that we, too, are fearfully and wonderfully made, beloved sons and daughters of the Most High. Mr. Van Wagenen's seed of faith enabled Sojourner Truth to plant her own, and Ms. Truth's faith that things could be different for her family and Black Neighbors compelled her to sow seeds of righteousness.

After Ms. Truth escaped from slavery, she learned that one of the children she had left behind, a five-year-old son, had been illegally sold across state lines. Her autobiography says she returned to the place where she had been enslaved to demand answers.

There, the wife of her former enslaver taunted her, saying, "Why, haven't you as many of 'em left as you can see to and take care of?"

Ms. Truth, however, was undeterred; she answered "in tones of deep determination––'*I'll have my child again.*'"

To which the woman replied, "Have *your child* again! How can you get him? And what have you to support him with, if you could? Have you any money?"

---

* Visit www.thecrownact.com/about to see if the CROWN Act has passed where you live.

As faith empowered her, Ms. Truth answered, "No, I have no money, but God has enough. . . . I'll have my child again."[20]

Later, she spoke of her courage: "I was sure God would help me to get him. Why, I felt so *tall within*—I felt as if the *power of a nation* was with me!"[21]

Indeed it was. With God on her side, assistance from the Van Wagenens, and faith in her back pocket, Ms. Truth got her son back. She also became a truth teller: an outspoken advocate for the rights of Black folk and women—particularly Black women. She delivered her powerful "Ain't I a Woman?" speech in 1851 at the Women's Rights Convention in Akron, Ohio. Ms. Truth, who was estimated to be around fifty at the time, walked to the front of the building and minced no words:

> The poor men seem to be all in confusion, and don't know what to do. Why children, if you have woman's rights give it to her and you will feel better. . . . I can't read, but I can hear. . . . The Lady has spoken about Jesus, how he never spurned woman from him, and she was right. When Lazarus died, Mary and Martha came to him with faith and love and besought him to raise their brother. And Jesus wept—and Lazarus came forth. And how came Jesus into the world? Through God who created him and woman who bore him.[22]

Ms. Sojourner Truth stood up for the truth because she had faith that all things were possible with God. She didn't know how long it would take for Black folk to be free or for women to be given full rights as human beings. But she stood up, spoke up, and exhibited acts of faith. She became heralded in American history as a bold orator who advocated for all women's rights. Beloved, we may not know how long it will take for policies, structures, and institutions to catch up. We may not know how our *stand up* will leave a legacy in communities, in cities, and in nations. But our *stand up* is critical, especially as we watch our Black Neighbors robbed of life and honor, right in front of us.

Confession: I didn't watch the footage of the May 25, 2020, killing of George Floyd at the hands of Minneapolis cops until the spring of 2021. I couldn't bear to watch it, and I stopped halfway, overcome by a torrent of sobs. On one video recording, I heard folks in the background, standing up to the officers. One said, "His nose is bleeding."[23] Another asked, "How long y'all gotta hold him down?"[24] Another said, "He is human, bro."[25] These witnesses to injustice called out what was wrong. An EMT in the crowd asked someone to take his pulse.[26] While their pleas didn't save Mr. Floyd's life, their words invited justice to roll down like a river.[27] Their public rebuke of the officers, coupled with the filming of the event, resulted in a twenty-seven-million-dollar wrongful death suit for Mr. Floyd's family.

Their *stand up* reminds people worldwide that *stand up* is critical, even if there isn't immediate change. Their *stand up* gives us the courage to speak the truth, even if—and especially if—our culture tells us to just trust authority. Their *stand up* ignited protests and marches in cities throughout the world, causing companies, organizations, and entire industries to examine how they treat their Black Neighbors. We don't yet know the full generational impact their *stand up* will have.

Ms. Rahab and Ms. Truth stood up for the future generations they envisioned. They lived by faith, but they never got to see the fullness of what they stood up for: "These all died in faith, not having received the promises, but having seen them afar off, and were persuaded of them, and embraced them, and confessed that they were strangers and pilgrims on the earth."[28]

While Ms. Rahab immediately saw her family saved when the Israelites overtook Jericho, she never got to witness King David's reign, as flawed as it was. Neither did she experience the coming of Christ. And while Ms. Truth lived to see slavery abolished in 1865, she never got to see Black men and women like herself receive the right to vote through the Voting Rights Act of 1965, more than one hundred years after she delivered her famous speech.

When grounded in faith, our *stand up* plants seeds of righteousness, seeds of God's kingdom here on earth. Sometimes it takes months, years, or many generations to bear fruit, but the seeds always bear fruit. Always. By choosing to *stand up* for your Black Neighbor today, you are planting seeds of righteousness that can bear fruit five, fifty, and five hundred years from now! You sow these seeds—not just so that righteousness can prevail in one instance with one person, but so that it can prevail throughout the land, from generation to generation. So that God's kingdom can reign here on earth, just as it does in heaven.

In the traditional Black church in the U.S., there's always been a constant gaze toward heaven because righteousness reigns there. The Black church has maintained this forward gaze—not just because of the injustice here on earth, but because of the infinite and eternal justice of our Father God in heaven. Black believers have always understood that justice and righteousness are the air we will breathe in heaven.

Black folk who've clung to the cross of Calvary amid an unjust world join the list of our faith ancestors in Hebrews who never got to see the fruit from the seeds they sowed. Folk like Ms. Sojourner Truth, Dr. King, and Ms. Harriet Tubman never got to see the fruit that would emerge from their *stand up*. Yet they planted the seeds and had faith that God would nourish and grow them.

*Standing up* is in your spiritual bloodline. It's a part of your spiritual DNA. Every time you speak up and *stand up* for your Black Neighbor, you join the list of faith ancestors who had so much faith in God that they acted on it even when the culture around them didn't. You can be counted among those who helped restore some of what was robbed back to your Black Neighbor. As you choose to love your Black Neighbor through your *stand up*, you sow seeds of righteousness.

## HEART CHECK

- Has there been a time you haven't stood up for your Black Neighbor? What stopped you from speaking up? How might you stand up for your Black Neighbor in the future?

- In what ways can you speak up or stand up for your Black Neighbor? Search your heart and ask the Spirit of Love.

- What steps can you take to stand up for your Black Neighbor this week? Write down the steps and be sure to do them.

### *Prayer Pause*

*Spirit of Love, as counterintuitive as it feels to ask to carry someone's burdens, I'm asking you to help me carry my Black Neighbors' burdens alongside you. Help me speak up and stand up for my neighbors, despite potential personal costs. Please help me to be shackled neither by fear nor by the culture of silence. Give me strong faith on which I can stand up for my neighbors.*

# CHAPTER 10

# The Black Love Lens: God's-Gifts

"Black Americans give a larger share of their wealth to charities than any other racial group in America."[1] This fact is so rarely reported that I'll quote it again: "Black Americans give a larger share of their wealth to charities than any other racial group in America."

In 2012, the W. K. Kellogg Foundation reported that Black households give away 25 percent more of their income per year than white households. That same report showed that Black households give $11 billion annually to causes and organizations.[2] While I'm sure these stats have changed slightly over the years, they are staggering, especially when you consider the racial wealth gap in the U.S. In 2021, the Board of Governors of the Federal Reserve System published an article about this gap, writing, "In the United States, the average Black and Hispanic or Latino households earn about half as much as the average White household and own only about 15 to 20 percent as much net wealth."[3]

*Did you catch that?* The average Black household earns only about half as much as the average white household, and Black households possess only a small fraction of the wealth of white households. Yet Black households give 25 percent more of their income than their white counterparts.

It's simultaneously encouraging and disturbing when you realize that the Robbed Ones have consistently chosen to be exceptional givers—all while being labeled "looters" and "robbers" throughout American history. There's something beautiful in Niger's descendants being willing to give—not necessarily from excess, but despite not necessarily having it.

In a 2020 series about race and inequality, *Washington Post* columnist Michelle Singletary reported that Black donors' giving "generally falls into three categories: 'Cornerstone' (giving to higher education and the arts), 'Kinship' (donating to organizations serving the Black community) and 'Sanctified' (supporting Black churches)."[4]

This rings true to me, as I can't remember a time when I wasn't encouraged to give. I remember giddily placing my quarter into the offering plate as a child, not recognizing that my parents gave me money to put into the offering plate every Sunday because they wanted to instill in me the value of giving early on. Through examples and encouragement, my family, church, and community taught me to give, which made giving a constant through line in my life.

I have joyfully gifted to others when I had a lot, when I had a little, and even when I had to dip into my savings. My community has always insisted that my neighbors—particularly Black Neighbors—are worth it and that the measure with which I gave would be the measure with which I would receive.[5] Back then, in the safety of my all-Black community, I didn't realize I was being taught to give God's-gifts—the fourth Black Love Lens.

God's-gifts are just that: gifts from God. They are resources that pass from God through us to our Black Neighbor. Gifts that are critical in light of the robbery our Black Neighbor has experienced. This robbery started in 1619, fossilized through slavery, shape-shifted in Reconstruction and the Jim Crow era, tormented through lynchings and assassinations, and siloed through segregation. This robbery persisted through redlining, underfunded public schools, and pay inequity and continues to steal, kill, and destroy through mass incarceration—or, as author Michelle Alexander put it, the New Jim Crow.[6] The robbery of our Black Neighbor can never be minimized or brushed aside as a relic of the past, because its poisonous tentacles live in our present.

In the midst of the robbery, God offers gifts designed to restore—financially, spiritually, emotionally, and relationally—what's been looted from our Black Neighbors individually and collectively. These gifts are so essential that we're gonna spend two chapters discussing them. This first chapter details what God's-gifts are, how they flow, and what it means to be a partner-in-love. The next chapter explains how we can become partners-in-love who gladly present God's-gifts to our Black Neighbors.

God's-gifts, delivered through us, embody God's love for our Black Neighbor. They sprout from divine roots and are demonstrated by us through acts of faith. God's-gifts are where divine provision for our Black Neighbor resides. You have the opportunity to join the Black community in doing what it has done so generously for centuries: sowing love into your Black Neighbor through God's-gifts.

## The Depth of God's Love

Before we talk about what God's-gifts look like in the everyday, let's take a step back to really understand this unique giving process God is inviting us into. Often, when we give, it's a two-party interaction: We give to someone else or someone else gives to us. Only two people are involved. This type of giving is one-dimensional and literally flat. The gift goes from point A to point B, with a potential thank-you involved, but that's it. Giving is done.

However, God invites us into a different kind of giving, a three-party interaction with dynamic movement where God's abundance of generosity overflows into every interaction: God gives resources to us, we give God's-gifts to our neighbor, God gives us joy through the interaction, and much more!

This multidimensional giving is profound. I don't want you to miss it, so let's get specific.

Let's say you feel a nudge to present a gift to your neighbor Kim. You may not necessarily know that she either needs or wants the gift, or even that she prayed for the gift, but you follow the Spirit's leading. When Kim receives the gift, she recognizes it was from God because it met a specific need, and she praises God because it came from him, albeit *through* you. Of course, Kim thanks you, too, because that's polite and appropriate, but God's love is the true star of the interaction because the gift originated from the heart of God. He provided for Kim's need, and so much more, out of the abundance of his love for her.

Through the exchange, Kim feels more seen and loved by God. You feel grateful that God's love was able to flow through you. Kim's trust that God provides for practical needs increases, as does yours. Your relationship with Kim grows as a result too.

## REPARATIONS

I've been asked if God's-gifts are reparations. The answer is two-fold: "Yes and no. No and yes."

"Yes" because God's-gifts house love and, by nature, love restores and repairs. So in a way, God's-gifts given to our Black Neighbors are a type of reparations, a way to help repair historic wrongs. I firmly believe that God seeks to restore what has been stolen from our Black Neighbors and that God's-gifts are one way this restoration happens.

"No" because God's-gifts are presents from God available to all our neighbors, regardless of whether historic wrongs have been committed against them or not. Also, reparations from governments and institutions may or may not house love.

Having said that, if reparations house God's love, then, yes, they are God's-gifts!

Reparations can be a type of God's-gifts, a way God's love flows to our Black Neighbors, but God's-gifts aren't always reparations.

With God's-gifts, it's never *just* about the money, the resource, or the act. God's focus is on the love that lies inside the gift. Love heals. Love restores. Like in the story above, God's multidimensional love is designed to care for the whole person, including their emotional, physical, financial, and spiritual needs. He wants to love our full person. And he's looking for partners-in-love to do the same for our Black Neighbors.

## Divine Wine from Partners-in-Love

John 2 shows one of the first demonstrations of God's love and provision for us in practical ways, and it's a beautiful illustration of a
partnership between Jesus and his mother.[7] The story takes place at
a wedding ceremony in Cana—it's Jesus's first miracle and a sneak
peek at God's-gifts in action.

Here's the scene: Jesus, his mom, and some of his disciples had
been invited to the festivities, but at some point during the event,
the host ran out of wine. I don't really drink, but I know that in
American culture, running out of alcohol at a wedding or any
other major social event is as bad as running out of food—maybe
worse! But in Middle Eastern cultures, it was downright shame-
inducing.

When Jesus's mother saw that the wedding host had run out
of wine, she told the hired workers to do whatever Jesus said.
She had faith that Jesus was gonna do his thang. And he did. After
the household staff filled up six large stone water jars, he turned
that water into wine. And this wasn't "two-buck Chuck" wine
you can grab at the local Trader Joe's. When the headwaiter tasted
the wine, he pulled the bridegroom aside and said, "Everyone
brings out the choice wine first and then the cheaper wine after the
guests have had too much to drink; but you have saved the best
till now."[8]

Jesus turning water into wine is widely viewed as a display of
his power, but it's also—just as importantly—a display of his and
his mom's love and concern for this family: that they would have
all they needed for their special occasion and that they would experience neither lack nor shame. Love for her neighbors motivated
Mary to ask Jesus to intervene, and her request was a type of prayer,

made in faith. Jesus responded to Mary's love and faith-filled prayer with a miracle. To most eyes, the wine was just very good wine, but (as cheesy as it may sound) it was divine wine, a God's-gift birthed from the Spirit of Love and Mary's act of faith.

The miracle at Cana yields another beautiful truth about God's-gifts: God prefers to work in partnership with ordinary people like you and me who have a lot or a little bit of faith. If Mary hadn't gotten involved, then that family wouldn't have received that miracle. Neither would they have experienced such a multidimensional and lavish display of love. Plus, Jesus's glory wouldn't have been put on public display.

During this ordinary wedding celebration, Mary became a partner-in-love. As such, she was privileged to peep a behind-the-scenes look at a miracle in the making. She got to witness Jesus make something extraordinary from something ordinary.

---

### GOD'S-GIFTS

*noun*

1. Gifts that the Spirit of Love invites people to give to fulfill specific needs or desires, showing the recipients that God cares for them physically, emotionally, and spiritually.

2. Gifts that are always *big*—not necessarily in size, but definitely in impact and love!

3. Gifts that are sometimes sacrificial and stretch our faith in God.

4. Gifts that sometimes feel extravagant because the Spirit of Love has a long history of giving lavish gifts.

## God's-Gifts in Everyday Life

Beloved, God is always looking for partners-in-love. How, then, can we become people who are willing to step into a partnership with an all-seeing, all-loving God? Practically, what does it even look like to be a conduit of love for our Black Neighbors?

To answer these questions, let's look at how God's-gifts can show up in our day-to-day lives. You ready? Because your mouth might drop. (Please note that the following numbers correspond to the definitions in the box above.)

### 1. God's-Gifts Meet Specific Needs or Desires

Sometimes your Black Neighbor will have a specific need or want (e.g., money, food, furniture, computer). They may or may not have voiced their desire, but the Spirit of Love knows the inner workings of their heart. When you feel the Spirit's nudge, confidently walk in faith that the Spirit is working through you to meet your Black Neighbor's very specific need. This happened to my friend Dewayne Smithers, who wrote about it on Facebook:

> In late 2013, I started believing God for a car, a debt-free car. The car, which is the Mustang I have now, showed up debt-free. It didn't come from a rich person, but from a single parent who lived in the cut in the hood.
>
> The car had been sitting in her parking lot for a year. Her exact words were this: "I don't know why but I feel deep in my heart that I'm supposed to give you this Mustang—free of charge." Two days later, I was driving a debt-free Mustang. No car payments. I didn't ask her for the car or make any hints about it. She was moved by God to do this.

Through this experience, God taught me a valuable lesson. We never know who God will use to bless us. It just may be someone struggling themselves. . . . You do the believing, and let God choose who He'll use to help you. He may surprise you.

Dewayne never told this woman about his prayer. He simply took his desire to the Spirit of Love, who in turn prompted the woman to give. That Mustang was from God! The woman was just a willing conduit of God's deep love and provision for Dewayne.

You, too, can be a conduit of God's deep love and provision for your Black Neighbor. Is there a resource you have that you feel God is asking you to give? Maybe it's not a car but an extra computer in the house or even a prized piece of art or furniture? As you look at your resources, begin a habit of praying over each item and listening to the Spirit of Love. Are you being asked to partner? If so, don't wait! Today, an ordinary day, is the time to witness God do something extraordinary!

*2. No Matter the Size, God's-Gifts Make a Big Splash*

In 2014, the Spirit of Love prompted me to host a party for Krystina, a young woman at my church who recently had been accepted into nursing school. I was excited for her, but we weren't close friends. So when the Spirit asked me to host a celebration for her, you wanna know what I did? I argued: "I'm not really close enough to her to throw her a party. That would be weird if I offered to do that for someone I don't really know that well. Besides, I just threw my sister, Bobbie Cheri, a party for her Grammy nomination,*

---

* Proud-big-sister moment and plug: Although my sister's song "Siempre Te Amaré" by Latin artist Frankie J didn't win the Grammy, you can listen to the song on your favorite music-streaming platform, cuz royalties are necessary for the success of songwriters like my sister.

so I don't have the money right now." I discarded the Spirit's prompting.

A few weeks later, Krystina and I were in a meeting at church. She told the group that she wanted to celebrate her acceptance into nursing school but she absolutely hated throwing parties. Immediately, I knew I needed to accept God's invitation to throw her the party, and I told her so. She was elated! Here's what she later told me about that experience:

I remember wanting to celebrate because it felt significant. I also wanted to not just have friends at the party but to have my mom and my dad as well. I wanted them to get a feel for my life in Southern California.

I love it when people gather, but I get stressed when hosting an event. I can remember my sixteenth birthday party: I had a panic attack during the party and after! I told myself, never again will I host a party! So when you offered, I was on cloud nine. It was an answer to prayer.

The event was great. I felt cared for and heard. You helped me get more in tune with what I really longed for and liked. I remember I wanted Ethiopian food, but there was a point where I felt, "Oh, that seems excessive. We don't have to do all that." But you encouraged me to be excessive, because that's what I really wanted. It was really powerful to me.

The entire event was a gathering of people from different spheres of my life. I remember my mom tearing up and being thankful that I was surrounded with such a great community of friends. I was warmly hosted that day, and it felt good. I was surrounded by family and close friends, so I didn't feel the need to perform or have things go a certain way, which meant no panic attacks!

More so, I was blown away that you even did it for me—still

am to this day. I grew so much from that experience. I learned how valuable it is to celebrate the way I want to celebrate, how powerful it is for someone to come alongside me to make my vision happen in real time. In fact, a few years later, I even started my creative birthday weekend ideas!

The party was truly God's-gift to Krystina: an idea birthed by God that flowed through me to my Black Neighbor. God showed his love for Krystina not just with the party. Her parents met her friends and church community, she was unburdened from party planning, she was able to own and express her desires, she celebrated a milestone in her life, and on and on and on! God's-gifts always contain much more than the gift itself. The Spirit of Love operates multidimensionally.

God invited me to be a part of that special day by organizing the party details. He didn't need me to have the financial resources to throw the party. He knew that the Grammy celebration had gobbled up my extra cash, and he already had a plan in place—Krystina's parents happily paid for our Ethiopian feast! God needed me to be a partner-in-love, willing to bend to my Black Neighbor's needs, so he could lavishly love her.

Are you willing to take a small step of faith to partner with Love? If God is nudging you to do something for your Black Neighbor, something that may feel small or slightly weird to you, take the leap of faith and do it. Then sit back, and watch what happens as you partner with God to love your Black Neighbor.

### 3. God's-Gifts Are Sometimes Sacrificial and Stretch Our Faith and Trust

When I worked for a faith-based organization in my early twenties, my salary was so low that I had to share a room, dorm-style, while I ministered to college students at USC. I was always on a tight budget—not only because of my minuscule salary but also because Los Angeles is notoriously expensive. One day, I drove one of my students, a young Black woman, to the grocery store. I picked up my items for the week, and she picked up hers, which consisted of multiple packs of Top Ramen and other food staples that broke college students often grab. When we got to the register, the Spirit of Love nudged me to pay for her groceries.

Although my heart wanted to say yes, my pocketbook screamed no. I didn't see how I could pay for both of us and pay for my groceries the following week. But I decided to accept the Spirit's invitation. And the next week, you wanna know what happened? Somebody brought extra pizza over to my house for dinner one night. Then someone else brought spaghetti after that. And day after day, folks gave me extra food. Suddenly, it didn't matter that I'd given away my grocery money. I had more than enough.

While God had given that student a gift through me, it felt more like a gift for me. I learned I didn't need to hoard my limited resources. If I gave willingly, the Spirit of Love would take care of me.

What about you? Do you sometimes say no to the opportunity to give because you fear you won't have enough? If so, take a moment to ask the Spirit to increase your faith and trust. He's got you.

### 4. God's-Gifts Are Extravagant Because the Spirit of Love Gives Lavishly

Beloved, when I say that God gives lavishly, I mean it. I experienced his overabundant love as a graduate burdened with college debt. Lemme tell you a story.

The first time I opened the guidebook to Pomona College, I fell in love. Ivy-covered buildings adorned lush, manicured lawns. A week or so after I received my acceptance letter, though, my father sat me down to talk about Pomona's equally lush price tag.

He essentially said, "We can't afford for you to attend Pomona."

He was right. Although he was consistently the top salesman at his Toyota dealership, my mother was a stay-at-home mom, and $30,000 a year for college was too steep.

$30,000 a year x 4 years = way more than we could afford!

Unfazed by the price tag, I looked my dad straight in the eye and said, "If God wants me to attend Pomona College, then God will pay for it."

I did attend Pomona College, and God did pay for it. I received tens of thousands of dollars in scholarships and grants, I worked a bit under work-study, my parents paid what they could afford each year, and the rest was taken care of by loans. Each semester, I would sign the loan papers, eyeing the numbers and the interest rate, knowing that I was indebting my future self to my present self. But it was worth it. Pomona was my dream school.

After I graduated, I decided to work at a faith-based non-profit. I didn't fully think about the consequences of working a low-wage job with $18,000 in student debt that would balloon to $30,000 over ten years if I paid the minimum monthly payment. But with such a low-paying job, the minimum was all I *could* pay!

About two years after I graduated, I called Pomona's financial aid office to see if I could reduce my interest rate.

"It's fixed," the woman on the phone told me, firmly but politely.

*Well, that didn't work,* I thought. I didn't know what else to do to avoid ten years of ballooning debt, so I dropped the idea and kept paying the monthly minimum. A few months later, I uttered words that would change everything.

I was sitting at my all-Black megachurch during the Sunday

night service when the guest preacher said, "Touch your neighbor, and testify about something God has done for you."

I turned to the woman next to me, touched her hand, and said, "God paid off my college loans!"

"When?" she asked, clearly surprised.

"I don't know!" I responded, equally surprised by the words that had come out of my mouth. They had just slipped out, kinda like when you've fallen in love with someone and accidentally say "I love you"—to their face—without planning to.

God hadn't paid off my loans, and I didn't even think that God *should* pay them off. When I had signed the loan documents for eight consecutive semesters in college, I knew full well the consequences, and I had agreed to them. God had also provided through scholarships and grants. He had already given enough; he didn't *owe* me anything.

However, God doesn't give us what is owed to us. God gives to us out of boundless, lavish love.

A month or so after I uttered this seemingly asinine testimony, I was having lunch with my play auntie* who flows in prophetic gifts. During lunch she said, "God is gonna pay off your student loans."

My mouth literally dropped open. I hadn't told anyone what I had said at church.

"And if it doesn't work out with one person paying it off," she added, "don't worry. Someone else will pay."

I told her about what I had testified at church during that Sunday night service. "Well, then," she responded. "Pray that God pays your college loans."

* A play auntie is a woman who is like family, or specifically like an aunt, to you. She's either a close family friend or a trusted member of the community.

Now it was abundantly clear to me. God wanted to pay off my student loan debt! But honestly, a part of me still doubted: *Could it really be true?*

Later that year, I was sitting down with one of my supervisors at work. At the time, our non-profit was actively looking for ways to help more staff of color be able to work and thrive within the organization. Finances were a huge part of that equation since everyone in the organization had to fundraise their ministry budget, which included their salary, and staff members from these oft underresourced communities were hit especially hard.

The conversation went something like this: "There's a donor who wanted to pay your college loans, but that donor fell through," my supervisor started. "But *other* donors stepped up and have agreed to pay your college loans for every year that you work for our organization."

*Insert the GIF where I slide out of my chair and onto the floor.*

I hadn't told my supervisor what I was praying for, yet here I sat with an overabundant gift from God lying in my lap. God filled in the financial gap neither me nor my parents could fill.[9] He answered my prayer through these donors' resources and care. I have no doubt they gave that specific gift because the Spirit of Love led them to. That's what the Spirit does: leads us to our neighbors' places of need.

## HEART CHECK

- Do you tend to hoard your resources (money, time, possessions)? If so, what are you afraid of?

- If you've ever said no to the Spirit prompting you to give to a neighbor, what was the result for you and your neighbor?

If you've ever said yes to the Spirit prompting you to give, what was the result for you and your neighbor?

## Prayer Pause

*Spirit of Love, I want to be a conduit of your love to my Black Neighbor. Please transform how I view money and giving. Help me become your partner-in-love that gives multidimensional God's-gifts. When you prompt me to give, help me give eagerly and with increasing love.*

# CHAPTER 11

# The Black Love Lens: God's-Gifts from Partners-in-Love

Can you imagine being a part of a community where people are eagerly giving away their homes, cars, or fancy designer handbags so that all your neighbors can be provided for? Well, that's what happened in Acts 4 when the early Christian church was growing exponentially. Thousands of people were embracing the message of the cross, home churches were flourishing, and a diverse group of believers met together regularly to hear Scripture and sing spiritual songs. This community was so enraptured by the resurrection message that they gave away their possessions so that those in need no longer experienced lack. They couldn't help themselves! Scripture says, "All the believers were one in heart and mind. No one claimed that any of their possessions was their own, but they shared everything they had."[1]

They were so united because "God's grace ['joy, pleasure, delight'[2]] was so powerfully at work in them all."[3] That joy was so strong that "there were no needy persons among them. For from time to time those who owned land or houses sold them, brought the money from the sales and put it at the apostles' feet, and it was distributed to anyone who had need."[4]

This scene was the natural outpouring of their love for God and love for one another. The believers were partners-in-love within their community. Can you imagine being so filled with God's joy that you view your resources as opportunities to serve your neighbors instead of as security blankets or markers of success? This scene in Acts demonstrates what's possible as we interact with our Black Neighbors and other neighbors.

But this joy fest took a tragic turn. A man named Ananias and his wife, Sapphira, sold a piece of property, like others had before them. But, instead of bringing all the proceeds to the apostles to give to their neighbors who had needs, they kept a portion of the money for themselves.

Sensing that Ananias had been dishonest, Peter essentially said, "Why have you lied to God by keeping part of the proceeds for yourself? Wasn't the property yours? And wasn't the money from the sale of that property yours too?"

Then Ananias fell to the ground and died.

A few hours later, Peter asked Sapphira if they had presented the entire amount, and unaware of what had just happened to her husband, she also lied. Then she died as well.[5]

This is one of the most tragic stories in the Bible because it was avoidable. God never asked Ananias and Sapphira to sell their property and give away the money. They made that choice, but their hearts weren't in the right place. Perhaps they wanted to *look like* they took joy in giving lavishly to God through the community. Perhaps giving felt like their religious duty, or perhaps, like the religion expert in the Love Samaritan passage, they wanted to justify themselves, to show everyone that they were righteous. While the story doesn't specify their motives for giving part of the proceeds and lying about it, we know their gift wasn't rooted in love for God or love for their neighbor. If it had been, Ananias and Sapphira would have given all the money. No shade, but they chose to be partners-in-lies instead of partners-in-love. The Spirit's response was clear: Better not to give at all than to lie to God and give with corrupt motives.

Wanting to be seen as partners-in-love who give lavishly without first allowing our hearts to be transformed by the Spirit of Love is tempting. Trying to do the right thing with the wrong motives is tempting. Imitating external faithfulness and congratulating ourselves for it is way easier (and, in the short term, more instantly gratifying) than cultivating interior faithfulness. Wrapping ourselves in wokeness is flashier than wrapping our Black Neighbor in sacrificial love. Publicly waving the banner of racial justice and reconciliation is easier than privately being crucified and transformed on the cross of Calvary. But that ain't the way of Love. Love sees the heart, and from Love all good gifts flow.

The members of the Acts community experienced an internal transformation. They first let God fill their hearts with joy and love, then poured out his love to their neighbors through God's-gifts. Because their motives were pure, their gifts became full of love—what I like to call "full giving." Conversely, Ananias and Sapphira's gift was devoid of the fullness of God's love, as are many of our culture's gifts. Their gifts fall flat—what I like to call "flat giving." Lemme explain.

Flat giving is purely transactional. When a person gives via flat giving, the giver or the recipient may have a positive experience, but that good feeling may not be felt by both. The resource is just that: a resource. An exchange of goods between two people, perhaps nothing more than donating clothes to the local Goodwill store and getting a receipt from the store clerk.

Full giving, on the other hand, is giving that is full of love and compassion. When you give from an outpouring of love and compassion, the resource exceeds its value and accomplishes more than it could otherwise. It becomes a multidimensional gift experienced by both the recipient *and* the giver. Full giving is a God's-gift.

To better understand this concept, let's narrow giving down to a specific resource—money—and watch it in action through the Love Samaritan.

When the Love Samaritan came upon the Robbed Man, he could've thought, *He's really hurt. I should help, but I gotta hurry up and get home. Lemme hurry up and clean up his wounds and take him to the inn so the innkeeper can take care of him. I'll leave some money there and he'll be fine.*

The Love Samaritan could've taken a hurried or detached approach to the situation and simply thrown money at the Robbed Man to try to fix his situation. The Robbed Man technically would've received the medical attention and financial resources he needed to heal. So yes, flat money is still money, and money gets stuff done, but money alone doesn't get done all that needs getting done. Flat money wouldn't have given the Robbed Man the love he needed to counteract the greed, selfishness, and utter disregard for his life that the robbers had displayed. Flat money would've been devoid of the Spirit of Love's care and concern. But that's not what the Love Samaritan did.

The financial resources the Love Samaritan poured into the Robbed Man—which included the money he left for the innkeeper, plus the money he lost from the time he spent away from his work—were full money. The Love Samaritan poured God's love into the Robbed Man. And as we know, love heals. Love restores. Because the Love Samaritan fully gave from the Spirit of Love, his gift was a part of the Robbed Man's internal and external healing. God's love was given multidimensionally and received multidimensionally. That's the nature of the full giving God wants us and our Black Neighbors to experience.

When your heart leans toward flat giving, you throw resources at a need without the strength of love undergirding your gift. At best, flat giving is devoid of love; at worst, it's filled with flattening agents like paternalism, guilt, social pressure, or a desperate desire—particularly when it comes to your Black Neighbor—not to appear racist. But when you lean into full giving, the Spirit of Love invites you into a multidimensional giving that grows the intimacy between you and God and between you and your Black Neighbor.

## REPARATIONS FOR A ROBBED COMMUNITY

In the summer of 1921, angry white mobs pillaged Greenwood, a Black community in Tulsa, Oklahoma, also known as the "Black Wall Street."[6] Hundreds of Black residents were murdered, and thousands of our Black Neighbors lost their homes and thriving businesses during the massacre. On the one-hundred-year anniversary of the Tulsa Massacre, the last three living survivors of that community—Ms. Viola Fletcher, 107; Mr. Hughes Van Ellis, 100; and Ms. Lessie Randle, 106—received God's-gifts through Pastor Michael Todd, lead pastor of Transformation Church in Tulsa. The church gifted each of them $200,000 in reparations and gave non-profits an additional $400,000 for a combined gift of $1,000,000.[7]

Pastor Todd told the crowd, "*Reparation* is not a political word. . . . Let me give you the definition of *reparations:* 'the action of repairing something that was devastated.' *Reparations* means that somebody is going to take up the mantle and actually put into action the process of repairing something that was destroyed."[8]

That's exactly what the church did. I believe they presented full gifts, full of God's care and compassion for a community that had been robbed of lives, homes, businesses, and any semblance of safety. These gifts were a reminder that although a century had passed, neither God nor their neighbors had forgotten them.

As Pastor Todd spoke to the survivors in front of an outdoor crowd, the joy and passion he felt while honoring his neighbors with God's-gifts were apparent. "I'm a young Black man who took over a church from a white man who built it in North Tulsa," he said. "That couldn't have happened if you all didn't survive. Today we can't restore everything that has been stolen from you. But today we can put a seed in the ground."[9]

That seed was love. Love sown into his Black Neighbors through God's-gifts.

## Full Giving from a Transformed Heart

The story about Ananias and Sapphira illustrates the importance of giving from the right heart posture, but how do you determine all that's motivating your giving? One way to examine your motives is to look at them in light of this scripture: "Each of you should give what you have decided in your heart to give, not reluctantly or under compulsion, for God loves a cheerful giver."[10] In other words, God loves when people give with wide-open hands and hearts. This posture is the barometer for every gift we give to our neighbors.

Let's say you come across a GoFundMe for one of your Black Neighbors or a fundraiser for an organization that serves Black youth, and you want to give. How do you know if it's a flat gift that's manufactured by pride, guilt, duty, or fear or if it's one of God's-gifts grown by love? To help, I've created reflection and prayer prompts to help you discern if the gifts you want to give are from a full heart.

First ask yourself a few questions:

- Are you excited to give? Does it incite joy?
- Does giving feel burdensome or compulsory?
- Does it feel like a purely transactional task?
- Do you feel proud that you want to give so generously?
- Are you looking forward to being acknowledged for your gift?
- Are you afraid to give because you might not have enough?

Then take a moment to allow the Spirit of Love to examine your heart's lens. Self-reflection is great, which is why I listed it as an initial step, but sometimes our hearts deceive us.[11] Sometimes we're inclined to think of ourselves more highly than we should.[12] The Spirit, however, can and will reveal the parts of our hearts we don't wanna see. So take a moment to ask the Spirit of Love what's motivating your giving. The goal is to give with pure motives and with joy. If your motivation is a sense of duty or obligation, then ask the Spirit to purify your motives. If you desire to save someone so you can be seen as the hero or heroine, then ask the Spirit to purify your motives.

When you pray, ask the Spirit of Love . . .

- to help you repent of—or turn away from—any impure motives.
- to reveal and deal with any selfish or ulterior motives.

- to reveal and remove any heavy burdens and obligations.
- to reveal and heal any fears around giving.
- to give you joy if you're being invited to give.
- to give you new lenses to give through.

Please know that as you pray about your motives, God will purify them. You will relate to your giving and your Black Neighbor through new lenses, and you will become more excited to give. You may find that you give even more! Remember that the goal is for love to flow through your resources. So give as you pray; pray as you give.

## Keep Pace with God

In 1 Chronicles, King David sat in his grand palace, enjoying the scenery, eating and drinking, loving life. As he sat, David had a startling discovery: He lived in the lap of luxury while God's treasure—the ark of the covenant, the seat of God—was under a tent. He said to Nathan, a prophet, "Here I am, living in a house of cedar, while the ark of the covenant of the LORD is under a tent."[13] Nathan heard David's lament and his desire to do the right and good thing—build a permanent home for God.

David's heart was in the right place, so Nathan co-signed David's plan, saying, "Whatever you have in mind, do it, for God is with you."[14] But that night, God spoke to Nathan and told him that David was *not* the one to build the temple. Instead, David's son Solomon would build the Lord's house. While his desire to give was coming from the right place, David's good gift wasn't his to give. But to know that, Nathan had to be in alignment with God's voice.

Giving is good. Praying about your giving is gooder (I know that ain't good English, but you get the point!). And when I say "praying," I simply mean talking to God about your giving: asking questions and responding to what you hear and sense. Only God knows the reasons, the gift, and the perfect time. Listen to God to ensure that the gifts you give are from his heart and mind and not just your own, however well intentioned. As my pastor Michael Koh says, "Keep pace with God." Run neither ahead nor behind but right alongside.

Several years ago, one of my friends, Dana, was struggling financially. Like many other artists, she was working in the service industry, taking acting classes, performing, but barely making ends meet. I was more than happy to give her a financial gift. Some months later, however, she was still stuck in the same financial rut. When I went to give her another gift, the Spirit of Love stopped me, saying, "No, I'm working."

I was surprised. The Spirit of Love had never told me *not* to give to someone. But I sensed that God wanted to do something in her heart as she struggled financially. I also sensed that once she received that internal gift, her financial drought would end. So I kept pace with God and waited.

Over the following weeks, I saw her faith and trust in God increase. Then she applied for and accepted a higher-paying job. While she held that job, she was able to work as an actor and pay all her bills with ease. Had I given my friend money, I would have interfered with the bigger plan God was engineering for her life.

Beloved, God loves when you are compassionate and willing to always give. However, he also wants you to be spiritually in tune to know when you are invited to present God's-gifts and when you are not.* Looking back, I see that as someone who loved her, I wanted to save Dana from her financial crisis. But I wasn't her sav-

* In his book *The Blessed Life,* Pastor Robert Morris shared some amazing stories about God's-gifts and offered new paradigms for how to view receiving and giving.

ior; she wasn't mine to save. Similarly, your Black Neighbor isn't yours to save.

Have you ever been tempted to believe that your Black Neighbor *needs* you and that it's your duty to save them? Have you ever grabbed your superhero cape and frenetically run ahead of Love? If so, now is a good time to drop your cape off at the Goodwill. (Better yet, trash it. We don't need other people out here tryna be heroines and heroes.) Instead, keep pace with God. Pray, and listen with a humble heart to hear where and how best to give. As you learn to discern and follow the Spirit's nudges, you will match God's pace.

You may be thinking, *Chanté, this sounds great. How does this actually happen? How do I hear God's voice? How do I know when to give and what to give?*

You hear God's voice—you learn what to give and when—by communing with God through prayer and Scripture. The more you talk to him, the more you commune with him in Scripture, the better you'll feel his gentle nudges. Recognizing God's nudges may feel out of your comfort zone. If so, don't fret; it takes practice. But until you've tuned your ear to his voice, I have five simple ways to discern if God is speaking to you:

1.  God's ways of doing things are often different from your way of doing things.[15] What you hear might be something you wouldn't have thought of on your own. Maybe it's something you kinda don't wanna do or are a little afraid to do. That's okay. Step out on faith!

2.  Pray alongside a trusted friend or mentor. If you feel like you're being asked to do something big or something that feels particularly risky, then have a spiritual mentor or spiritually mature friend pray alongside you. When the Spirit asks me to do something big—like write a book or move to

another city—I always pray with trusted friends and family because if the Spirit is speaking to me, the Spirit will most likely tell someone else in my community as well.

3. Read God's Word regularly to strengthen your connection to God's voice. As you read more and more about God in Scripture and become familiar with his voice, you will be able to more easily discern God's voice when you're not reading Scripture.

4. The Spirit will never say anything that conflicts with Scripture. The Spirit's nudges always align with what God has already said. So, if you think you sense the Spirit inviting you to steal from the rich to give to the poor, know that it ain't the Holy Spirit talkin' to you!

5. Test it out. Sometimes the only way to know if the Spirit is speaking to you is to simply do what you heard. Sometimes you won't know if you've heard correctly until you act and see what happens! "Test it out" is a great motto to adhere to when you're new to trying to keep pace with God. Testing out small things, like the nudge to buy someone a cup of coffee, will give you confidence to do bigger things down the road.

Keeping pace with God as a partner-in-love is a lifelong adventure. We get to listen to and follow the Spirit's nudges and be a part of a divine outpouring of love. So let's start with the fundamentals to learn how to intentionally practice hearing God speak about something we all use every day: money.

Every time you receive extra money, whether it's a bonus, government refund, or settlement payment, instead of buying something superfluous or saving or investing those funds, pause. Then ask the Spirit of Love if you should gift all or part of it to one of your Black Neighbors. If Love shows you a specific person or group to give to, then give. If Love doesn't say to give, then tuck it away to give on another occasion. Keep listening until the occasion arises. Trust me, the occasion *will* arise.

Or if you really wanna grow as a partner-in-love, then do this every time you receive a paycheck. When you cash your paycheck or as that automatic deposit hits your bank account, take a prayer pause to ask Love if there's a Black Neighbor you can give to.

Honestly, you may not always know for certain if the Spirit of Love is inviting you to give a specific gift, but you will learn the feel and voice of the Spirit over time as you step out on faith. Love, like faith, has legs.

## Where God's-Gifts Mingle

Until now we've talked about God's-gifts being given away, outside of commerce, but God's-gifts can also be given and received within the marketplace, flowing from God through you to your Black Neighbor.

I always look for ways to love my Black Neighbors in the marketplace. I work with Black hairstylists, makeup artists, and photographers, and I purchase my bath and body products and African-inspired clothing from Black-owned businesses. Also, I try to buy as many books as possible from independently owned Black bookstores instead of Amazon. At times, I have to pay more for these items because they are sold by small-business owners instead of big-box retailers, but love is worth the cost.

When I was putting together my professional team—my literary agent, talent agent, CPA, and bookkeeper—I wanted to hire as many Black people as possible, and I prayed specifically that God would bring the right people whom I could sow into and who would really see me and support me. And they do. They believe in my talent, support my vision, call to check on me, and sometimes pray for me. I feel their love and care for me through their work. And I communicate my care and love for them through thank-you notes and gifts and by praying for them.

Yes, these are business relationships where I have hired them to perform specific services, but God's-gifts are in action because the money is flowing from God through me to them, and love, joy, prayer, and gratitude are flowing all around. Our relationships aren't purely transactional; they're steeped in service, partnership, and love. In scenarios like these, when full giving is present, God's-gifts become an avenue to establishing and strengthening intimacy. Because when you reimagine the marketplace as a place where God's-gifts can be exchanged, then you'll find a place where Black Love Lenses mingle.

A 2019 report commissioned by American Express found that "African American women-owned businesses represented the highest rate of growth of any group in the number of firms between 2014 and 2019."[16] Despite this high rate, a study conducted by *Harvard Business Review* found that "only 3% of Black women are running mature businesses"—those that have survived for more than five years. Researchers cited many potential factors contributing to this disheartening stat, including less support from investors, fewer bank loans, and reduced personal capital because of college debt, underscoring the fact that "access to key resources needed for entrepreneurship are unevenly distributed in U.S. society, reinforcing the advantage of certain groups while impeding the entry and catching-up of disadvantaged groups."[17]

CNBC recently reported on the racial wealth gap in the U.S., saying that in 2022, "for every $1 of wealth held by a white family, a Black family had just $0.25."[18] Among the culprits cited for this wealth disparity were homeownership rates and business ownership rates, both of which stem from unjust policies and lenses that have robbed our Black Neighbors from centuries past to the present day. So by investing God's-gifts in Black-owned businesses, we can help the marketplace become a more equitable, loving place for our Black Neighbors.

When God directs you to give in the marketplace, it becomes a place for you to intentionally *stand up* in support of your Black Neighbors. God is showering your Black Neighbor with love through his gifts and providing you with the opportunity to *stand up* for her by investing in her business as a customer, angel investor, business mentor, resource connector, and more. The marketplace is an optimal place for the power of your *stand up* to intersect with the power of God's-gifts.

---

Looking to *stand up* for a Black-owned business? The following directories provide business listings.

**Official Black Wall Street**—https://obws.com
From diverse products to brick-and-mortar restaurants, this site connects you with Black-owned businesses throughout the U.S.

**EatOkra**—www.eatokra.com
EatOkra promotes restaurants that celebrate the culinary richness of the African diaspora.

**BLK + GRN**—https://blkgrn.com
BLK + GRN is "an all-natural marketplace by all Black artisans" created to provide access to non-toxic personal care products and to fund Black female entrepreneurs.

**ByBlack**—http://byblack.us
ByBlack lists Black-owned businesses in select U.S. cities.

How will you partner with Love to shower your Black Neighbors with God's-gifts? Perhaps you will give the bonus you receive at work, buy gourmet coffee from a Black-owned business, or even pool funds with friends and family so you have a larger pot from which to give. The possibilities for how to give are endless, so have fun and get creative!

Your gifting doesn't need to be perfect. You may have hiccups and missteps along the way. But set your heart toward God, tune your ears to his voice, and match his pace. As you do, you will grow into a strong partner-in-love for your Black Neighbors over time. Eventually you will be so deeply rooted in Love that you automatically give lavish God's-gifts without thinking about it, just like the members of the early church in Acts. When that happens, you will be a partner-in-love who unassumingly presents full gifts to your neighbors from a full heart.

## HEART CHECK

- Think of the times you've given to your Black Neighbor. Have you sometimes given out of guilt or shame or for appearance's sake? Has your giving been rooted in the fullness of the Spirit of Love? If needed, take a moment to confess.

- How do you feel about keeping pace with God in relation to your giving?

- When you think about growing as a partner-in-love who gives lavishly to your Black Neighbor, is a part of you fearful that God is a taskmaster who will demand the most precious thing? If so, confess your feelings and ask for a new lens to see Love through.

## Prayer Pause

Think about and list all your resources: your financial resources, your natural resources (land), your human resources (skill set), your possessions, and so on. Once you've made the list, take a moment to pray over each item on it. Then listen to Love's response. Write down anything you hear, and then go give it! If you don't hear anything now, no worries! Eventually Love will show you exactly what to give.

*Spirit of Love, I thank you for this list of resources in my care. I recognize that these resources are yours, not mine. And that you have plans for each one. Please open my eyes and my heart. Prepare me to be a partner-in-love with you. As I read each item on this list, reveal any gift that you want me to present to my Black Neighbor from you.*

*God, is _____ a God's-gift to my Black Neighbor?*

&lt;Pause to listen.&gt;

# CHAPTER 12

# The Black Love Lens:
# The Spirit of Love

Can't nobody do me like Jesus.
> —"Can't Nobody Do Me like Jesus"
> by Rev. James Cleveland

Scripture unequivocally teaches that giving is good and you should give generously.[1] Yet the best gifts are personal rather than generic, because the best gifts are rooted in the deepest love. No one loves like the Spirit of Love. Like we say in the Black church, "Can'tNobodyDoMeLikeHim!" Because we recognize that nobody—not even our mamas—can love us the way God loves us. I want to illustrate this with a story that shows the fifth Black Love Lens—the Spirit of Love—in action.

In the spring of 2019 during my daily prayer time, I felt the Spirit of Love nudge me to pray for my friend Ava, an Afro-Latina. Specifically, that she not be anxious. I had never known Ava to be a particularly anxious person, but I prayed against anxiety anyway. After I finished praying, I almost called her to check on her, but I didn't know how to start the conversation. What was I supposed to say? "I feel like God was showing me that you're anxious. Uh, are you anxious?" If she wasn't, then I'd look like some sort of spiritual weirdo. So I didn't call.

The next day, while I was praying, the exact same thing happened. I sensed the Spirit of Love asking me to pray that Ava not be overcome by anxiety. Again I prayed against anxiety, and this time, I called her to check in. *Wanna know what happened?*

Turns out that, for the prior few days, Ava had been experiencing deep anxiety. She had even experienced panic attacks, the first in her life. As she told me the story of why she had become anxious, I listened, feeling her pain. I marveled at how God loved Ava so much that he supernaturally told one of her friends what she was struggling with so she could have emotional support from a beloved neighbor and so her struggle could end. I asked Ava to share what that experience was like. Here's what she told me:

> I've felt anxiety before but have never battled with it. So when my anxiety rose and the panic attacks hit, I knew I was struggling. I was scared, and the situation felt out of my control. I was trying to pray, but to be honest, I've never been somebody who prays deeply. So I prayed a quick one-and-done prayer: *God, I need your help with this.*
>
> Then you came to me and told me God put me on your heart to pray for something so specific as anxiety. I felt heard; I felt valued at how specific, how completely invested, how absolutely obsessed God is with me—in the best way possible. I am his. Every waking thought and every issue about me is so important to him. Nothing is too small, and he will not have his daughter bound. My understanding of how God values me and where I am in his heart was renewed.

The Spirit of Love knows your Black Neighbors intimately. Every need, every thought, every whisper of their hearts, is known. When you open your heart and ears to hear the Spirit of Love in prayer, you can experience supernatural insight that is personal and timely.* Your prayers open the gate for the Spirit of Love to shower your Black Neighbors with specific and timely love through the Black Love Lenses.

## Loving Through Love's Lenses

The Spirit of Love empowers the other four love lenses and works through them. From the Spirit comes the humility we need to bend to our Black Neighbors, to honor, and to foster intimacy. From the Spirit's leading, we draw the courage to stand up for and the insight to present God's-gifts to our Black Neighbors. When we understand this, we're compelled not just to seek to love through these lenses but foremost to ask for the Spirit, whose love extends beyond the other four love lenses by holding infinite love and insight into our Black Neighbors. As we cultivate intimacy with the Spirit, we are automatically connected with that love and insight.

To better understand how the Spirit of Love gives us insight to love with specificity and timeliness, I want to turn to photography for a moment. I love how, in photography, the lens you use to take pictures makes all the difference. The lens can be the difference between a blurry image of a jump shot and an image of the game-winning shot that graces the cover of *Sports Illustrated.*

In the summer of 2022, Ken Fong, wildlife photographer and director and host of *Asian America: The Ken Fong Podcast,* posted on

---

* I'd be remiss not to mention that Pastor Michael Koh always speaks about the Spirit being timely.

social media a stunning picture of a hummingbird drinking water from a Japanese bamboo fountain.[2] The photo was so sharp that you could see the hummingbird's beak as it drank from the bamboo spigot. I mean—you could see the individual drops of water! The details were amazing. On top of the clarity, the vivid colors popped on the screen. The hummingbird's green-and-yellow coat and the golden-yellow bamboo tube, both set against the purple bougainvilleas blurred in the background. The blend of colors was a feast for the eyes that would normally go unnoticed.

When I saw the photo and read that Dr. Fong was able to capture the shot only because he purchased a special lens, I immediately thought of what happens as the Spirit of Love shows us details through prayer. So I set up a phone interview with Dr. Fong to understand how he captured the shot. He and his wife had installed a Japanese rock garden in their backyard the prior winter, complete with a traditional *tsukubai* basin and bamboo fountain. To his delight, hummingbirds visited to drink from it during the summer's torrid heat. He said,

> I wanted to capture a hummingbird drinking from the fountain, so I ended up sitting about twenty feet away inside our patio. I have an Olympus 150–400mm (that's the focal length) telephoto zoom lens, which allows me, depending on how small or big the object is, to fill more of my viewfinder with the tiny bird. This specialized long-reach lens allows you to do the number-one thing of wildlife photography—fill as much of the viewfinder as possible with the creature that you're trying to capture.[3]

*Did you catch that?* Dr. Fong used a super-telephoto zoom lens so the hummingbird filled his viewfinder. If you're like me, perhaps you're scratching your head and wondering why that matters. Well . . .

The long lens that Dr. Fong used was so powerful that it allowed him to capture the hummingbird as if he were right next to it, rather than twenty feet away. The lens essentially reduced the physical space between him and the hummingbird. Through that lens, the hummingbird's magnificence filled the entire viewfinder, and Dr. Fong could see details about the bird he couldn't ordinarily see with the naked eye.

Likewise, prayer is how the Spirit of Love gives us a spiritual telephoto zoom lens to see our Black Neighbor. As we pray, the Spirit can show us specifics about our Black Neighbor through the Spirit's long lens. We can see with a sharpness not always possible with human lenses, helping close the space between us.

Loving your Black Neighbor with the Spirit of Love is like seeing them through the Olympus 150–400mm lens. Loving your Black Neighbor without the Spirit of Love is like seeing them through a Polaroid camera lens. The Spirit of Love longs to give you a crystal-clear, sensitive lens that allows you to love your Black Neighbor with a specificity that causes their mouth to drop open, just like Ava's. The Spirit is always looking for people willing to love with new lenses.

## A Person of Prayer

One of the primary ways you learn to love like Love is through prayer. Prayer is just talking to God, giving God space to talk back, and partnering with God to do what you heard. Prayer is sitting with God so that your heart can be examined. Prayer is where inevitable compassion for your Black Neighbor lives, where compassionate long-suffering grows. Prayer is a precious place where you receive new lenses.

As you pray consistently, through "joy and pain, . . . sunshine and rain,"[4] you recognize the Spirit's nudges and voice in every moment of the day—not just when you're praying or reading Scripture, but when you're folding laundry, watching a movie, and shopping at the grocery store. As Pastor Michael Koh likes to say, you become "a person of prayer." You'll know because prayer will become the through line of your life. As you transform into a person of prayer, the Spirit empowers you to love your Black Neighbor in the specific ways she needs to be loved, which will grow your love multidimensionally. This happened between my friend Meagan and me.

Before I tell you the story, first I must tell you a secret about me: I keep the clothes that I really like until they develop holes and start to fall apart. For example, I wore the full-body slip my mother bought for me when I was thirteen into my late twenties. It wasn't until after the little pink floret at the top of the slip fell off and a hole opened in its place that I thought, *Maybe I should throw this away.* Even then, I waited five years to actually throw it away.

So when the hot-pink robe embossed with my initial C started to amass holes after about six years of consistent use, I just kept wearing it. For one, it was still functional. Second, my good friend Sarah had gifted it to me for being a bridesmaid in her wedding, so it had sentimental value. Plus, I was in the struggling-artist phase of my career, suffering from an inconsistent paycheck. Because of this and a scarcity mentality, I clung to what I had for fear I wouldn't be able to afford a replacement.

But for months, God had been inviting me to have faith that I would be taken care of and to live in abundance. As I looked at the tattered bathrobe one summer evening, I decided to throw it away and believe that God would replace it with something just as beautiful, something hole-less! So I thanked the robe, Marie Kondo–style, for its presence in my life and threw it away as an act of faith.

My birthday was a few weeks later, and I gifted myself what I gift myself each birthday: a yummy brunch and trip to the beach to reflect on the previous year. Even though I didn't host a celebration, my friend Meagan bought me a gift. When I opened the box, inside it sat a pink robe. Clutching the robe to my chest, I exclaimed, "I needed one of these! How did you know?"

"It was interesting," Meagan replied. "When I got to the store, I asked God to show me what to buy you, and then I felt directed to the robe section and to this robe," she added. "But you can exchange it for another, if you want."

There was no need to. It was perfect. A pink robe to replace a pink robe. Proof of God's abundant love for me and proof that the Spirit of Love loves personally and is always on time.

The robe was an example of Meagan loving me, her Black Neighbor, with one of God's-gifts. She prayed, and then the Spirit of Love led her to the robe. Had she not prayed and instead just bought what she figured I'd want, like a Starbucks gift card, it would've been an ordinary gift. Yes, I would've been grateful (cuz any day is a good day for a latte), but the gift wouldn't have had the same impact because it didn't come from the Spirit of Love. When Meagan prayed for direction on how to love her Black Neighbor, the Spirit honored her heart and allowed her to love me with specificity through the Spirit's lens.

You can practice this daily with your Black Neighbors. One of my mentors says that each morning, after she's compiled her to-do list, she stops and prays over it, asking the Spirit if there's anything she should change or add. Likewise, as you're preparing for the day (or the next day if you prepare the night before), you can ask the Spirit if there's a specific way you can show love to your Black Neighbors that day. Then listen and respond. Some days you may hear something, and other days nothing, and that's okay. The simple practice of prayer will grow you into a person of prayer and someone who can love their Black Neighbors intentionally and more deeply.

So far, we've talked about how the Spirit of Love can engage us in prayer as we love our individual Black Neighbors, but what about the Black community—our collective Black Neighbors? How can we love them through prayer? We love our Black Neighbors through intercessory prayer empowered by the Spirit of Love.

Simply put, intercessory prayer is praying to God on behalf of someone else. You can intercede in prayer alone, but I've found increased strength and power in numbers. The complex web of racism, oppression, dishonor, unjust policies, silence, restrictive covenants, greed, pride, and the like that seek to perpetually rob the Black community needs intercessory prayer.

## Loving Your Black Neighbors Through Intercessory Prayer

In his online class "Understanding the Fight Against Slavery," scholar and teacher Dr. Richard Bell asked about racism, "How do you slay a many-headed monster?"[5]

That's the question sociologists, historians, activists, clergy, and many others have asked for decades. The sobering answer is "Not easily, not alone, and not without the power of Love."

The vestiges of slavery, Jim Crow, and subjugation are too deeply imprinted on our culture for them to be removed easily. Your resolve alone isn't strong enough to defeat the many-headed monster that is racism. Your mind isn't smart enough to brainstorm how to undo the impact of more than four hundred years of racial oppression. Your inspired charitable giving isn't potent enough to right every wrong. Even collectively, we aren't savvy enough or inventive enough to figure out how to completely dislodge racism from systems, structures, and individuals' lenses.

Only the Spirit of Love, who has infinite insight and power, can show us how to move mountains and slay monsters. Through prayer, the Spirit of Love gives us the force of Love to withstand and fight the forces of racism.

We need the force of Love.

In the book *Prayer Is Invading the Impossible,* the late pastor Jack Hayford poetically described the axis-shifting prayers the community of believers in Acts boldly prayed:

> *Violence.*
> *Life breaking into the strongholds of death.*
> *Light driving darkness into the corners.*
> *Love.*
> *Love without gushiness.*
> *Love without fear.*
> *Loving violence. Violent lovingness.*[6]

There's a strange, almost-poetic irony in the fact that, like love, prayer can be gentle and violent. A mother is gentle with her newborn baby, but if you try to harm that baby, her love will prove violent. God's love for our Black Neighbors is gentle, but when racism comes to wreak all manner of havoc on them, love gets violent. Not in a "cut your ear off" sort of way, but in an "I've come to slay the monster of racism" sort of way. It's the same with prayer. As Scripture says, "Our struggle is not against flesh and blood, but against the rulers, against the authorities, against the cosmic powers of this darkness, against evil, spiritual forces in the heavens."[7] Our fight against racism is spiritual. To confront it, we must *stand up* for the Black community in prayer. Hour after hour, day after day, month after month, year after year.

My mom often talks about the tarrying services she participated in at the COGIC church she attended as a teenager. They would go to the altar at the front of the church, bend down on their knees, and tarry (wait) for the Spirit for as long as it took. They would sing spiritual songs, pray, and tarry until they felt the Spirit's presence, heard the Spirit's voice, and felt power from on high. They often tarried for hours, receiving more and more from the Spirit the longer they waited in prayer.

Although American culture has been described as a fast-paced microwave society, racism in our land won't be overcome by sporadic microwave prayers uttered by a few people. Our Black Neighbors—or any of us, for that matter—won't be free from the shackles of racism until legions of us tarry in intercessory prayer for God's reign of love and justice.

In January 2023, I was researching the section of this book where I talked about the Confederate monuments being removed. I had started my workday like I normally do—with breakfast and prayer—and afterward it was time to write. As I was reading news articles to prepare to write, something strange happened. My body started to shake. I started sobbing uncontrollably. I lost the ability to type a single word. In my eight years of writing about race, nothing remotely like this had ever happened. It felt as if I was directly encountering the evil force that is racism. It shook me, physically and emotionally. As I sat on my couch, heaving sobs, I immediately knew that alone I was no match for the formidable force I felt. So I texted and emailed the intercessors who were praying for this book and asked them to pray alongside me. They did, and a few hours after they prayed, I was able to resume my work, no longer shaken. In this instance, it didn't take long for our collective prayers to push the spiritual darkness away.

Sometimes, though, intercessory prayer is a labor of love that must happen over an extended period. Sometimes intercessory prayer is like being in the desert, desperate for water, and digging and drilling and drilling and digging—however long it takes—until you hit water. In our case, intercessory prayer for our Black Neighbors is drilling and digging in prayer until the robbery ceases and justice and righteousness flood our land. It is drilling and digging in prayer—past powerful forces, past fear, past pain, past disillusionment, past anger, past exhaustion—until we finally reach living water. The only water that can sustain us and the seeds of righteousness we've planted in the ground.

Beloved, don't grow weary as you pray for justice and righteousness to rain down on our land. You will reap a harvest if you don't give up.[8] Remember, the spiritual battle you encounter through intercessory prayer is a marathon. One your spiritual ancestors started running long ago. Like in any race, without the proper refreshments, your energy and strength will wane.

If you engage in prayer as an action step in pursuit of racial justice but neglect to care for and refresh your spirit, then you will find you don't have enough strength in and of yourself. You will burn out. Or become bitter. You may even become physically violent because the Spirit of Love will no longer be your anchor. However, the Spirit longs to fill you with the force of Love, to fill your reservoirs and strengthen you.

As you dig in prayer, let the Spirit replenish you through spiritual songs and Scripture. Worship and communion will refresh you and remind you of God's goodness and power to defeat any enemy.

As the Spirit refreshes, you will receive the strength of an unflinching love that can face every *ism* and impossibility with courageous faith.

I recently reread *A Wrinkle in Time* by Madeleine L'Engle. In the story, thirteen-year-old Meg Murry sets off on an epic adventure to find and save her father, a scientist who has gone missing. With the help of three celestial-like beings who serve as guides, Meg, her brother Charles Wallace, and their friend Calvin embark on a head-spinning journey that changes how they view time, travel, and what's possible in the physical world. During their travels, Mrs. Who, one of Meg's guides, gives Meg a pair of glasses with special lenses that can rearrange atoms and do things deemed impossible.

IT, the book's evil antagonistic force, controls people's thoughts, words, and actions. Everyone controlled by IT seems to march to the beat of IT's pulsating brain, somehow collectively doldrummed into IT's rhythm. Yet, whenever anyone wearing the glasses encounters IT, they don't feel the full force of its destructive power. The lenses shield the person wearing them from the full impact of evil.[9]

The Spirit of Love does the same for us as we take the time to tarry in prayer for our Black Neighbors. We receive special lenses that enable us to not be overcome and overwhelmed by racism and its monstrous tentacles. As we tarry in prayer, we receive strength. God trains our hands for battle, and our arms can bend bows made of bronze.[10] And like Meg does at the end of the book (spoiler alert), we too can *stand up* to evil. We can *stand up* to the evil that is racism through prayer with the full force of Love undergirding us.

When we unite in order to love the Black community through prayer, then Love can swoop in to slay the many-headed monster of racism. As you engage in this current era of racial reckoning, I hope you remember that the Spirit of Love is a force to be reckoned with. I hope you look to our spiritual ancestors from the civil rights movement and beyond who boldly protested and insistently prayed that our Black Neighbors be loved. I encourage you to refresh your spirit like the protestors who sang prophetic songs as they marched, because, Beloved, "we shall overcome someday."[11]

## Love in Action: Putting It All Together

If you feel a desire to pray more or become a person of prayer, then act on that desire. Decide how and when you will pray. Be sure to put it on your schedule so you don't forget, whether it's while you're driving to work, during your lunch break, or when you awake in the morning. If you're new to prayer, then maybe you start off by praying for fifteen minutes, then increase to thirty minutes, forty-five minutes, an hour. . . . You can keep going! There's no limit!

Do you want to commit to praying for your Black Neighbor with a group? If so, carve out time to pray with your family, church community, or friends. For more than three years, I've prayed with my mom's side of the family (her mom, her sisters, and their children) weekly. Every Sunday at 5 P.M., we meet via FaceTime to pray for what's happening in our lives and in our land. These prayer times have grown our family spiritually and strengthened our connection. You can do something similar. Find the prayer warriors in your life who want to join arms with you to pray for your Black Neighbor.

Set aside time to pray, either individually or collectively, on a weekly, monthly, or quarterly basis for a specified amount of time. You may decide to pray monthly for one year and then reassess at year's end if you're able to continue the following year. Or maybe you want to commit to praying annually during each day of Black History Month. Choose a time frame that excites you and that you can commit to.

When the time comes to pray, begin by singing spiritual songs and focusing your attention on God. Then, as you feel still and focused, create space to pray for your Black Neighbors. Did something happen in the news? At work? If you're new to intercessory prayer, then start by praying for justice and righteousness for your Black Neighbors in one specific place (your local school, neighborhood, church, city, etc.). Follow the Spirit of Love's leading to where your Black Neighbors need prayer support. Consider listening prayer—pray for specific guidance, and listen to see what the Spirit shows you to pray for. Then dig.

Remember to refresh your spirit as well. Allow love to fill your reservoirs for the marathon before you. One of my friends, Jenny, used to set aside every Tuesday as her "healin' and dealin' day," where she would intentionally focus on seeking healing through therapy and prayer for various issues she was dealing with. Similarly, my friends Pat and Sarah periodically carve out time for each of them to go on two-day prayer retreats where they can meet with the Spirit and pray apart from their five kids. Whether it's two days, one day, or one hour, give the Spirit space to refresh you. The opportunity to allow God's love to flow through you to your neighbors is too critical to allow anything to block it.

Whether you are digging in prayer or asking for specificity, the Spirit wants to close the space between you and your Black Neighbors. Love wants to give you the right lenses to see and love your Black Neighbors. Love wants to endow your prayers with power from on high. So as you seek to love your Black Neighbors by honoring them, experiencing intimacy with them, giving them God's-gifts, and standing up for them, be sure to love them through prayer.

## HEART CHECK

🔍 What is your relationship to prayer like?

🔍 Have you ever experienced disappointment and heartbreak
because you prayed for something that didn't happen? If so,
has a part of you turned cold toward prayer and God as a result? If this is the case, then ask the Spirit to heal your heart
and give you the desire and courage to pray again.

🔍 Has fighting for justice for your Black Neighbors left you
feeling tired and burned out? Or maybe angry and disillusioned? If so, ask the Spirit to refresh you. Carve out time and
space to be replenished.

### Prayer Pause

*Spirit of Love, I want to experientially understand the
power of prayer. Please help me cultivate intimacy with you
by praying more and becoming a person of prayer. Show
me how to see and love my Black Neighbors through your
lenses. Give me the strength to dig in prayer until I see justice and righteousness reign in our land.*

# PART THREE

# Go and Do Likewise

# "Lift Every Voice and Sing"

Lift every voice and sing,
Till earth and heaven ring,
Ring with the harmonies of Liberty;
Let our rejoicing rise
High as the list'ning skies,
Let it resound loud as the rolling sea.
Sing a song full of the faith that the dark past has taught us,
Sing a song full of the hope that the present has brought us;
Facing the rising sun of our new day begun,
Let us march on till victory is won.

—James Weldon Johnson[1]

CHAPTER 13

# Transforming the Road

The road from Jerusalem to Jericho described in the Love Samaritan passage was so dangerous that it was known as the Ascent of Blood because of "the blood which is often shed there by robbers."[1] On April 4, 1967, Dr. Martin Luther King, Jr., delivered his sermon "A Time to Break Silence" at Riverside Church in New York City. He spoke about how we can interact with this dangerous road. Although Jesus clearly invited us to be the Good Samaritan to our Black Neighbors, Dr. King knew our love couldn't end there: "We must come to see that the whole Jericho Road must be transformed so that men and women will not be constantly beaten and robbed as they make their journey on life's highway."[2]

Dr. King's words ring true to this day. Not only are we asked to love our Black Neighbor who has been injured on the road; we must also transform the road itself. To learn how to do this, we will look at a few examples from history to the present day that shed light on how we can repair the road that enables our Black Neighbor to be robbed continuously.

In 1832, underwhelmed by the lackluster educational opportunities at schools for "Colored" people, Richard Humphreys left 10 percent of his estate to establish a school where Black residents of Philadelphia could receive a formidable training as teachers.[3] His will asked thirteen fellow Quakers to start the school.[4] Mr. Humphreys wanted to provide steady job opportunities for his Black Neighbors. An added benefit was that trained Black teachers would lavish their Black students with the love, encouragement, and educational opportunities most of their white counterparts wouldn't. Research has shown that Black teachers hold higher expectations for Black students than their white counterparts. In addition, Black students who have at least one Black teacher by the third grade are more likely to graduate from high school and attend college.[5]

Established in 1837, the Institute for Colored Youth, later renamed Cheyney University of Pennsylvania, became the first HBCU in the U.S.[6] An exhibit about the university, hosted in Falvey Library at Villanova University, noted that in the institute's early days, "Most graduates went on to teach in schools in both the North and the South. Others became physicians, government employees, lawyers, and business owners."[7]

Although the school was small in those early days, boasting only about a hundred students twenty-five years after its start, its leaders believed the seed they were planting was valuable, regardless of how big it grew. Their 1864 annual report read, "All that this single school may accomplish may seem to be but as a drop in the bucket, yet we are not therefore to shrink from putting forth our best efforts, though the educational labors of those we send out may reach but a limited number among the millions in this nation."[8]

Though the start was small, the impact has been mighty. Cheyney University has blossomed into a school that has graduated more than thirty thousand college students over its nearly two-hundred-year history, while withstanding numerous obstacles. Just as beautiful is the reality that, even from his grave, Mr. Humphreys worked to transform the road, leaving behind a legacy of love whose ripples are felt to this day.

Jasmin Shupper, president of Greenline Housing Foundation, wants to leave this kind of legacy as well. Through her work, she hopes to "restore what centuries of housing discrimination have broken for people of color."[9]

Her organization's mission is "to close the racial wealth gap and homeownership gap and reverse the effects of systemic racism in housing by using grants as a form of up-front equity."[10] In addition to providing grants for down payments, Greenline Housing Foundation offers home maintenance grants and financial education to qualified people of color.

The idea for the non-profit emerged in early 2020 after Ms. Shupper tried to figure out how to bring about justice for her Black Neighbors who were routinely subject to discrimination and brutality. She remembers grieving and praying, "Lord, I wanna do something, but who am I? I'm only one person."

Then she heard the Spirit whisper, "Use who you are and what you have, with where you're at."[11]

And that's exactly what she did. She used her experience as a real estate agent and former insurance agent to *stand up* in faith for her Black Neighbors.

Greenline is changing the road "by facilitating access to home-ownership, by giving reparations in the form of a grant," she says. "Greenline and the work that we do is really restorative and re-demptive in nature. We want to help people establish and leave an economic legacy for their families."[12]

Ms. Shupper is transforming the road for her Black Neigh-bors alongside Greenline's board and its partners, which include churches, private institutions, individual donors, and real estate professionals.

Now the question is, Which part of the road is the Spirit of Love asking you, your family, and your community to repair? Will it be in government? In your neighborhood and city? In your church's community development programs? At your local school?

A lot of times Love invites us to love right where we are, using what we already have, even if it feels small. Ms. Shupper used her knowledge of insurance and real estate. Mr. Humphreys used his money. Over the last several years, I've used my pen.

## Road Repair

In early 2019, I read a news article about how the state of California had introduced the CROWN Act. *Wait. What?* I thought. *How has natural Black hair become a civil rights issue?* I did some research and eventually wrote an article for JSTOR Daily titled "How Natural Black Hair at Work Became a Civil Rights Issue."[13] Published on the fifty-fifth anniversary of the Civil Rights Act, the article traced the history of discrimination against natural Black hair in the U.S., citing how courts had ruled on the topic.

Writing the article was a way for me to advocate for myself and my Black Neighbors, a way to repair part of the road. I didn't know the article was a seed that would grow.

Over time, the article spread throughout the country and has been cited in legal cases by the ACLU of Connecticut and in law journals like *Virginia Law Review* and *Harvard Journal of Law & Gender*. It is a part of the diversity curriculum for one of the largest school districts in the U.S. and is a trusted resource used by teachers and social justice organizations across the country.

I get teary-eyed every time I think about the impact of that article. How could I have known, while sitting in my home office, that my words would be used to affirm my Black Neighbors? To remind them that how God made them and their hair is beautiful and worthy of legal protection. I didn't have to travel the country or learn a new skill to write that article. I planted that seed from my home, using the talents God gave me, and have begun to see it grow to transform the road. Just like my friend, educational consultant Dr. Queenie Johnson.

In 2019, Dr. Johnson created Black School, a pop-up school that provides opportunities to dialogue, develop a strong identity, and build cultural leadership skills for Black students ages twelve to nineteen. Soon thereafter, Dr. Johnson created Black School for White People, a global leadership training platform designed to help racial justice-seekers dismantle anti-Blackness and transform systems. Her schools are changing how people think and live. Dr. Johnson educates her students about the condition of the road and how they can repair it. The seeds teachers plant in students reach far and wide—into every space where those students reside. Imagine the impact one of her students can have on the people they lead and the places they live. Imagine the influence ten of her students can have on people and places. Now imagine thirty, fifty, a thousand. The reach of the seeds she's planted is boundless. These stories remind us that we can repair the road now, in our spaces of influence. Our seeds can grow over time.

## Loving Alongside

Throughout my life, my mother, Vivi, has been a pillar of faith and constant model of what it means to love your Black Neighbor as yourself. I've watched my mom present God's-gifts to her Black Neighbors, when she had plenty and when she had little. I've watched her use her culinary training to cook up free dinners for the Black students I worked with post-college. I've also watched my mother pray for her Black Neighbors, be it 5 a.m. or 5 p.m.—no time was off limits. As a result, I've learned to do the same. I've given sacrificially to my Black Neighbors, cooked up soul-food dinners for students, and interceded. (But honestly, it's more like 5 P.M. cuz I ain't no early riser!)

For more than a decade, I watched my mother house young women who needed a place to stay. Some stayed for months, others for years. When a family friend, Ruth, asked if we could house a pregnant woman from her church who didn't have a place to live, my mom and I said yes. We welcomed her into our family home and showered her with Love's grace and compassion. That yes meant days and nights interrupted by a baby's wails, but we counted it better to honor this woman and her child with love and kindness than to receive a peaceful night's rest.

My mom isn't a super saint. She's just a faith-filled woman who said yes to Jesus's invitation to love her neighbor as herself. Looking back, I realize that my mom has been imparting a legacy of love to me throughout my entire life. I'm learning how to love my Black Neighbors as I watch and serve alongside her.

God created us to be communal beings, to love and learn shoulder to shoulder. So invite your family to love your Black Neighbors alongside you. Grow as partners-in-love with your spouse, parents, cousins, friends, and community. Teach your children, godchildren, nieces, and nephews—*all* the children you love. Plant seeds, love your Black Neighbors through new lenses, repair the road, and leave a legacy of love—*together*.

## HEART CHECK

What part of the road do you feel excited to repair?

What tools and skills do you have that could help transform the road?

- Who can you invite to repair the road alongside you?

- In what specific ways can your family love your Black Neighbors and transform the road?

- Take a moment to dream about the type of love legacy you and your community could leave.

## Prayer Pause

*Spirit of Love, I want to be a repairer of the road for my neighbors. Would you show my family, my community, and me where exactly to work and pray? Would you strengthen our resolve to see the road transformed, despite how long it takes? Would you water our small seeds so they can leave a legacy of love?*

# CHAPTER 14

# "Stony the Road We Trod"

Imagine yourself sitting on a bench at a park in your neighborhood. You're hunched over on the bench, grieving everything you've read throughout this book. You're upset and perhaps disillusioned at the extent of the robbery your Black Neighbor has experienced, and maybe you're trying to wrap your mind around your own sins. Imagine yourself sitting with whatever emotions you've encountered while reading this book.

Imagine Jesus coming to you, putting his arms around you, and applying wine to your wounds. Then imagine Jesus administering oil (the Holy Spirit) to you. Imagine Love's presence wrapping you like a warm cashmere blanket.

Now sit with Love.

When you're ready, stand up and imagine taking a walk on the road to Jericho.

When you see your Black Neighbor on the side of the road, go to him and do likewise.

# ON CHANTÉ'S SHELF

Here's a list of some of the books on my bookshelf.

**Recommended Reads**

*Be the Bridge: Pursuing God's Heart for Racial Reconciliation* by Latasha Morrison

*The Color of Compromise: The Truth About the American Church's Complicity in Racism* by Jemar Tisby

*Fortune: How Race Broke My Family and the World—and How to Repair It All* by Lisa Sharon Harper

*Healing Racial Trauma: The Road to Resilience* by Sheila Wise Rowe

*How to Be Less Stupid About Race: On Racism, White Supremacy, and the Racial Divide* by Crystal M. Fleming

*Let Us Pray* by Watchman Nee

*Prayer Is Invading the Impossible* by Jack Hayford

*Reading While Black: African American Biblical Interpretation as an Exercise in Hope* by Esau McCaulley

*So You Want to Talk About Race* by Ijeoma Oluo

*A Sojourner's Truth: Choosing Freedom and Courage in a Divided World* by Natasha Sistrunk Robinson

*Then They Came for Mine: Healing from the Trauma of Racial Violence* by Tracey Michae'l Lewis-Giggetts

*Why Are All the Black Kids Sitting Together in the Cafeteria? And Other Conversations About Race* by Beverly Daniel Tatum

## To-Read Pile

*All the White Friends I Couldn't Keep: Hope—and Hard Pills to Swallow—About Fighting for Black Lives* by Andre Henry

*Becoming Brave: Finding the Courage to Pursue Racial Justice Now* by Brenda Salter McNeil

*The Black Presence in the Bible: Discovering the Black and African Identity of Biblical Persons and Nations* by Rev. Dr. Walter Arthur McCray

*His Name Is George Floyd: One Man's Life and the Struggle for Racial Justice* by Robert Samuels and Toluse Olorunnipa

*How Africa Shaped the Christian Mind: Rediscovering the African Seedbed of Western Christianity* by Thomas C. Oden

*A Just Mission: Laying Down Power and Embracing Mutuality* by Mekdes Haddis

*The New Jim Crow: Mass Incarceration in the Age of Colorblindness* by Michelle Alexander

*The Power of Group Prayer: How Intercession Transforms Us and the World* by Carolyn Carney

*Raising White Kids: Bringing Up Children in a Racially Unjust America* by Jennifer Harvey

# ACKNOWLEDGMENTS

It takes a village to write a book, and I'm grateful for every person in my village. Fam Bam—Mom, Grandma Ruby, Auntie Cheryl, Bobbie Cheri, Kim, Nicole, Carly, Cherayne—thank you all for praying for me and encouraging me every step of the way. (Also, shout-out to Jaylen, Kevin, and Donnell for your support.) A huge thank-you to Dad, Mona, Grandma Ruthie, Grandpa Bobby, Grandma Julie, and all my extended family for offering prayers and encouraging words. Auntie Renae, thank you for encouraging me to ask for what I wanted and for helping me assemble my team.

I also thank everyone who watered this book when it was just a seed: Ed and Marcia Ollie, Kathy Khang, Vanessa Carter, Roger Freet, and the Publishing in Color Conference.

My deepest thanks to my Patreon and prayer partners who gave when the Spirit asked, spoke words of encouragement, and prayed incessantly: Pat and Sarah Ku, Ernie and Salome Chung, Amy and Andrew Kenny, Aidan Lewis, Sonia Balcer, Chuck and Yvonne Jones, Steve and Larissa Marks, Brett Jaxel, Cori Esperanza, Ryan and Teresa Ku, and Michael and Christie Stalcup.

A rousing round of applause for my literary agent, Jevon Bolden of Embolden Media Group, for championing this book, introducing me to amazing editors and publishers, and assisting with every aspect of production—from the initial proposal to the marketing copy. Huge props to Sharifa Stevens for providing editorial support in the developmental stages and helping me see the manuscript with fresh lenses.

Cue the marching band for my wonderful editor, Kimberly Von Fange! Kim, thank you for being my prayer partner, skilled editor, sounding board, encourager-in-chief, sometimes-counselor, and, when necessary, ghostwriter. I'm also hugely indebted to the entire WaterBrook and Penguin Random House teams. A special shout-out to the team that crafted the cover: photographer Yemi Kuku, painter Keshad Ife Adeniyi, and the entire graphic design team that put it all together. Also thanks to editorial assistant Luverta Reams and to Laura Barker for believing in this book and me.

I'm grateful for every person who endorsed this project. Thank you for generously giving your time, energy, and words. Thanks to everyone who shared their stories and expertise, whether you were named or unnamed in the book: Bishop David Daniels; Darrin Rodgers; Dr. Cecil M. Robeck, Jr.; Jasmin Shupper; Dr. Ken Fong; David and Grace Eze; Rey and Glen Sirakavit; Jenny Hall; Kat Negrete; Krystina Daniels; and Kristal Adams.

Special thanks to those who read portions or all of this manuscript during its draft stages: Elder Oscar Owens, Sean Watkins, Juanita Butler, and John Lew. Unending thanks to my dear friends who offered encouragement over the years: Camille-Kay Brewer, Canden Webb, and Dr. Feven Negga. And loving thanks to the other two members of the Faithful Trio: Dr. Ebony Boyce Carter and Dr. Dalila Zachary.

Pastor Michael Koh, thank you for modeling what it means to become a person of prayer and for your impact on this book. A big thanks to other VCFers: Cindy Koh, Scott and Sara McKey, Jose and Mary Alvarez, Betsy Stewart Jackson, Kim Thomas-Barrios, Shannon and Ashantha Rubera, Ms. Mona, and so many others. You all held my arms up.

Thank you to all the Black Binders, including Grace Sandra, Jodi M. Savage, Dr. Cynthia Greenlee, Heather McClean, Tyrese Coleman, TaRessa Stovall, Almah LaVon, Tiffany McCreight, Dr. Stephanie Andrea Allen, Shannon Luders-Manuel, Adiba Nelson, Tracey Michae'l Lewis-Giggetts, Sheila Wise Rowe, and Patricia Raybon. Thank you for supporting me and for offering invaluable advice on agents and publishing.

Thank you to every member of Freedom Road's Global Writers' Group: Lisa Sharon Harper, Marlena Graves, Andre Henry, Anna, Barbara, Ashley, Stephen, Sara, and everyone else who provided invaluable feedback.

Thanks also to others who supported this project: Velynn Brown, Bernadette Hengstebeck, James Yu, and Dorina Lazo Gilmore-Young. Plus, the incomparable Mrs. Rosemary Jenkins, my honors English teacher, who instilled a love for the English language in my marrow. Thank you to everyone who received book email updates and to the team at Belnano Coffee. Thank you, Mr. Boyd, for providing insight about the Black Love Lenses and for the beautiful butterfly effect you've had on my life.

Also, huge props to my team! Thank you to my agents at the Polygon Group who graciously gave me time off from auditioning and performing to write. Jacqueline and Meredith Lewis, thank you for providing the financial glue for this project and my writing business. Last, a big thank-you to the California Arts Council for granting me an Individual Artist Fellowship to help fund this book project. (Please note that the council doesn't necessarily support the book's contents.)

To the Kinnears—Jennifer, Guy, Ian, and Sophia—thank you for being my home away from home. Thank you for cooking for me, praying for me, listening to my rants, and welcoming me into your home and hearts as your first "artist in residence." You provided me the physical and emotional space necessary to write a book of this magnitude. You are living examples of what it means to love your Black Neighbor as yourself.

Last, the biggest thank-you to the Spirit of Love. Thank you for entrusting me with the idea for this book back in 2006 and for the adventure we've been on the last eighteen years. It's an honor to know you and to be loved by you.

# NOTES

## Before You Begin

1. C. H. Woolston, "Jesus Loves the Little Children," Hymnary.org, https://hymnary.org/text/jesus_loves_the_little_children_all_the.

2. "Movin' On Up (Theme to The Jeffersons)," by Ja'Net DuBois and Jeff Barry, Songfacts, www.songfacts.com/lyrics/janet-dubois-and -oren-waters/movin-on-up-theme-to-the-jeffersons.

3. *Jerry Maguire,* directed by Cameron Crowe (Culver City, Calif.: Tri-Star Pictures, 1996).

4. Janelle Harris Dixon (@thegirlcanwrite), Twitter, April 26, 2016, https://twitter.com/thegirlcanwrite/status/725013706103525376.

5. "What Is Hashem?," My Jewish Learning, accessed August 18, 2023, www.myjewishlearning.com/article/hashem.

6. 1 John 4:7–8.

7. Ibram X. Kendi, "Ibram X. Kendi Defines What It Means to Be an Antiracist," Penguin Books Limited, June 9, 2020, www.penguin .co.uk/articles/2020/06/ibram-x-kendi-definition-of-antiracist.

## Chapter 1: Love Yourself

1. Deuteronomy 6:5.

2. Luke 10:27.

3. "Open the Eyes of My Heart," by Paul Baloche, PraiseCharts, accessed August 18, 2023, www.praisecharts.com/songs/details/1724 /open-the-eyes-of-my-heart-sheet-music.

4. Ithiel C. Clemmons, *Bishop C. H. Mason and the Roots of the Church of God in Christ* (Largo, Md.: Christian Living Books, 1996), 45.

5. Clemmons, *Bishop C. H. Mason,* 58.

6. Daniel K. Norris, "How Azusa Street Exposed—and Overturned—

Racism in the Church," Charisma News, October 11, 2016, www
.charismanews.com/opinion/from-the-frontlines/60462-how
-azusa-street-exposed-mdash-and-overturned-mdash-racism-in
-the-church.

7. Norris, "How Azusa Street."

8. G. B. Cashwell, quoted in Dr. Cecil M. Robeck, Jr., "The Past: Historical Roots of Racial Unity and Division in American Pentecostalism," 17, www.pctii.org/cyberj/cyberj14/robeck.pdf.

9. Ijeoma Oluo, *So You Want To Talk About Race* (New York: Seal,
2018), 22.

10. Robin DiAngelo, *White Fragility: Why It's So Hard for White People
to Talk About Racism* (Boston: Beacon, 2018), 14.

11. Proverbs 6:16–19.

12. 1 Peter 4:8, NLT.

13. 1 Corinthians 13:7.

14. 1 Corinthians 13:7.

15. Hebrews 12:1.

16. 2 Thessalonians 3:13, NKJV.

17. Matthew 9:12; Mark 2:17; Luke 5:31.

## Chapter 2: Robbed of Love

1. Latifah Muhammad, "White Man Drags Black Passenger Suffering
Seizure off Metro Train in California," Vibe, August 5, 2018, www
.vibe.com/news/national/white-man-drags-black-man-seizure
-metro-train-599879.

2. Luke 10:26–29.

3. Luke 10:29.

4. Luke 10:29–37.

5. Martin Luther King, Jr., "I've Been to the Mountaintop" (sermon,
Mason Temple, Memphis, Tenn., April 3, 1968), www.american
rhetoric.com/speeches/mlkivebeentothemountaintop.htm.

## Chapter 3: Love Withheld

1. *Boyz n the Hood,* directed by John Singleton (Culver City, Calif.:
Columbia Pictures, 1991).

2. Luke 10:29–37.

3. Encyclopedia.com, s.v. "Purification: Purification in Judaism,"

accessed August 21, 2023, www.encyclopedia.com/environment
/encyclopedias-almanacs-transcripts-and-maps/purification
-purification-judaism.

4.  Leviticus 21:1–6.

5.  Leviticus 15:11–20.

6.  2 Corinthians 5:21.

## Chapter 4: Love Poured Out

1.  Luke 10:29–37.

2.  "Strong's G3708—Horaō," Blue Letter Bible, accessed August 22, 2023, www.blueletterbible.org/lexicon/g3708/niv/mgnt/0-1.

3.  "Strong's G4697—Splagchnizomai," Blue Letter Bible, accessed August 22, 2023, www.blueletterbible.org/lexicon/g4697/niv/mgnt /0-1.

4.  Don Stewart, "Why Is the Holy Spirit Associated with Anointing with Oil?," Blue Letter Bible, accessed August 22, 2023, www .blueletterbible.org/Comm/stewart_don/faq/the-identity-of-the -holy-spirit/29-why-is-the-holy-spirit-associated-with-anointing -oil.cfm.

5.  Joy DeGruy, *Post Traumatic Slave Syndrome: America's Legacy of Enduring Injury and Healing,* rev. ed. (Portland, Ore.: Joy DeGruy, 2017), 105.

6.  John 14:13–14.

7.  Luke 10:36.

8.  Luke 10:37.

9.  Luke 10:37.

10.  "Strong's G4160—Poieō," Blue Letter Bible, accessed August 23, 2023, www.blueletterbible.org/lexicon/g4160/niv/mgnt/0-1.

11.  Matthew 3:10, kjv.

12.  Matthew 7:18, kjv.

13.  1 John 4:7, nkjv.

## Chapter 6: The Black Love Lens: Intimacy in Neighborhoods

1.  "The Declaration of Independence—1776," United States Code, Office of the Law Revision Counsel, accessed August 24, 2023, https://uscode.house.gov/download/annualhistoricalarchives/pdf /OrganicLaws2006/decind.pdf.

2.  Luke 10:31–32.

3.   "Los Angeles, CA," Mapping Inequality: Redlining in New Deal America, The Digital Scholarship Lab, accessed August 24, 2023, https://dsl.richmond.edu/panorama/redlining/#loc=11/34.005/-118.212&city=los-angeles-ca.

4.   "Los Angeles, CA: A59," Mapping Inequality: Redlining in New Deal America, The Digital Scholarship Lab, accessed August 24, 2023, https://dsl.richmond.edu/panorama/redlining/#loc=9/33.68/-118.418&city=los-angeles-ca&area=A59&adview=full.

5.   Dictionary.com, s.v. "restrictive covenant (n.)," accessed August 24, 2023, www.dictionary.com/browse/restrictive-covenant.

6.   "Los Angeles, CA: C161," Mapping Inequality: Redlining in New Deal America, The Digital Scholarship Lab, accessed August 24, 2023, https://dsl.richmond.edu/panorama/redlining/#loc=13/33.865/-118.532&city=los-angeles-ca&area=C161&adview=full.

7.   William H. Frey, "Even as Metropolitan Areas Diversify, White Americans Still Live in Mostly White Neighborhoods," Brookings, March 23, 2020, www.brookings.edu/articles/even-as-metropolitan-areas-diversify-white-americans-still-live-in-mostly-white-neighborhoods.

8.   "Let's Talk: What Is Redlining and How Does It Affect the Homeownership Gap Today?," Conversation Ally, September 15, 2020, www.ally.com/stories/home/what-is-redlining-how-does-it-impact-communities-today.

9.   Mapping Inequality: Redlining in New Deal America, The Digital Scholarship Lab, accessed August 24, 2023, https://dsl.richmond.edu/panorama/redlining/#loc=5/39.1/-94.58.

10.  *Underwriting Manual: Underwriting and Valuation Procedure Under Title II of the National Housing Act* (Washington, D.C.: Federal Housing Administration, 1938), paragraph 937, www.huduser.gov/PORTAL/sites/default/files/pdf/Federal-Housing-Administration-Underwriting-Manual.pdf.

11.  Ta-Nehisi Coates, "The Case for Reparations," *The Atlantic,* June 2014, www.theatlantic.com/magazine/archive/2014/06/the-case-for-reparations/361631.

12.  Julian Glover, "Black California Couple Lowballed by $500K in Home Appraisal, Believe Race Was a Factor," ABC7 News, February 12, 2021, https://abc7news.com/black-homeowner-problems-sf-bay-area-housing-discrimination-minority-homeownership-anti-black-policy/10331076.

13. Tenisha Tate Austin, quoted in Glover, "Black California Couple."

14. *Shelley v. Kraemer* was strengthened by the federal Fair Housing Act of 1968, which prohibited discrimination in housing based on race, national origin, or other factors. "The Fair Housing Act," Civil Rights Division, U.S. Department of Justice, June 22, 2023, www.justice.gov/crt/fair-housing-act-1.

15. The racist language of restrictive covenants is still in many property deeds throughout the U.S. In fact, until 2022, after Illinois passed Public Act 102-0110, homeowners in the state weren't allowed to remove the racist language from their property deeds. Sadly, this is a reality across many U.S. states. Kelsey Vlamis, "A New Law Lets Illinois Homeowners Remove Racist Language from Deeds, Including Clauses Saying a House Can Never Be Sold to Black or Jewish People," Insider, January 22, 2022, www.insider.com/new -law-lets-illinois-homeowners-remove-racist-language-from-deeds -2022-1.

16. "Representations of Black Women in Hollywood," Geena Davis Institute on Gender in Media, accessed August 25, 2023, https:// seejane.org/research-informs-empowers/representations-of-black -women-in-hollywood.

17. Chanté Griffin, "Blackness on the Margins: What Ann M. Martin Asked of Jessi in The Baby-Sitters Club," Literary Hub, August 2, 2021, https://lithub.com/blackness-on-the-margins-what-ann-m -martin-asked-of-jessi-in-the-baby-sitters-club.

## Chapter 7: The Black Love Lens: Intimacy in the Church

1. "Religion and Congregations in a Time of Social and Political Up- heaval," PRRI, May 16, 2023, www.prri.org/research/religion-and -congregations-in-a-time-of-social-and-political-upheaval.

2. Jemar Tisby, *The Color of Compromise: The Truth About the Ameri- can Church's Complicity in Racism* (Grand Rapids, Mich.: Zonder- van, 2019), 53–54.

3. African Methodist Episcopal, www.ame-church.com.

4. Tisby, *Color of Compromise,* 52.

5. Dr. Cecil M. Robeck, Jr., "The Past: Historical Roots of Racial Unity and Division in American Pentecostalism," 29, www.pctii.org /cyberj/cyberj14/robeck.pdf.

6. David Daniels, interview with author, Zoom, July 13, 2023.

7. Darrin Rodgers, interview with author, Zoom, June 22, 2023.

8.  Daniels, interview with author.

9.  Robeck, "The Past: Historical Roots," 31.

10. Robeck, "The Past: Historical Roots," 33.

11. Daniels, interview with author.

12. "AG USA Adherents by Race: 2001–2022," Assemblies of God, May 3, 2023, https://ag.org/-/media/AGORG/Downloads/Statistics/Attendance-and-Adherents/Adherents-by-Race-2001-through-2022.pdf.

13. Daniels, interview with author.

14. "Members of the Church of God in Christ," Religious Landscape Study, Pew Research Center, 2014, www.pewresearch.org/religion/religious-landscape-study/religious-denomination/church-of-god-in-christ.

15. Daniels, interview with author.

16. Eboni Marshall Turman, in *The Gospel According to André,* directed by Kate Novack (New York: Magnolia Pictures, 2018).

17. Robert Morris, "Pastor Robert Morris—a Lack of Understanding," GatewayChurchTV, October 14, 2017, video, 34:08, October 21, 2017, www.youtube.com/watch?v=kcNXWpk7Pbw.

18. Romans 12:15.

19. "14 High-Profile Police-Related Deaths of U.S. Blacks," CBC, December 8, 2017, www.cbc.ca/news/world/list-police-related-deaths-usa-1.4438618; "50 Black Women Have Been Killed by U.S. Police Since 2015," Insider, accessed August 26, 2023, www.insider.com/black-women-killed-by-police-database-2021-6.

## Chapter 8: The Black Love Lens: Honor

1.  "5091. Timaó," Bible Hub, accessed August 26, 2023, https://biblehub.com/greek/5091.htm.

2.  Matthew 15:8.

3.  Matthew 15:4; 1 Timothy 5:3, nkjv.

4.  There are an estimated one thousand to two thousand languages spoken on the continent of Africa. "Introduction to African Languages," The African Language Program at Harvard, Harvard University, accessed August 27, 2023, https://alp.fas.harvard.edu/introduction-african-languages.

5.  Oprah Winfrey (@oprah), Instagram photo, January 28, 2021, www.instagram.com/p/CKnIxQFB6L9/?igshid=3ampe8md0cc0.

6.  John 13:3–7.

7.  John 13:3.

8.  John 13:8, NKJV.

9.  John 13:8, NKJV.

10. John 13:12–16, NKJV.

11. "Strong's G3784—Opheilō," Blue Letter Bible, accessed August 27, 2023, www.blueletterbible.org/lexicon/g3784/kjv/tr/0-1.

12. Luke 10:37.

13. "Strong's G4160—Poieō," Blue Letter Bible, accessed August 28, 2023, www.blueletterbible.org/lexicon/g4160/niv/mgnt/0-1.

14. Timothy Bella, "Yale Honors Black Girl Who Was Reported to Police as She Sprayed Lanternflies," *The Washington Post,* January 31, 2023, www.washingtonpost.com/nation/2023/01/31/bobbi-wilson -spotted-lanternfly-police-yale.

15. Jason "Jah" Lee, "GTFOHWTBS: White New Jersey Man Calls Cops on 9-Year-Old Black Girl for Spraying Pesticide Because She 'Scared' Him," Bossip, November 11, 2022, https://bossip.com /2188553/new-jersey-man-calls-police-on-9-year-old-black-girl -for-spraying-bugs.

16. Vanessa Romo, "Yale Honors the Work of a 9-Year-Old Black Girl Whose Neighbor Reported Her to Police," NPR, February 4, 2023, www.npr.org/2023/02/03/1154049233/yale-honors-9-year-old -black-girl-neighbor-reported-police-lanternfly.

17. "Cross-Racial Identification and Jury Instruction," Innocence Project, May 20, 2008, https://innocenceproject.org/news/cross-racial -identification-and-jury-instruction.

18. Drew Harwell, "Federal Study Confirms Racial Bias of Many Facial-Recognition Systems, Casts Doubt on Their Expanding Use," *The Washington Post,* December 19, 2019, www.washingtonpost .com/technology/2019/12/19/federal-study-confirms-racial-bias -many-facial-recognition-systems-casts-doubt-their-expanding -use.

19. Sebastian Murdock, "White Woman Threatened to Call Cops on 8-Year-Old Girl Selling Water," HuffPost, June 26, 2018, www .huffpost.com/entry/white-woman-sees-black-girl-selling-water -allegedly-calls-police_n_5b2e94a5e4b00295f15cf35f.

20. "Outrage over Neighbor Calling Police on Grass-Cutting Kids Helps 12-Year-Old's Summer Business," *USA Today,* July 2, 2018,

www.usatoday.com/story/news/nation-now/2018/07/02/grass
-cutting-police-called-maple-heights-ohio/750760002.

21. Romans 12:10; Philippians 2:3.

## Chapter 9: The Black Love Lens: Stand Up

1. Luke 16:10.

2. Sojourner Truth and Olive Gilbert, *Narrative of Sojourner Truth* (Mineola, N.Y.: Dover, 1997), 20–21.

3. Isaac Van Wagenen, quoted in Truth and Gilbert, *Narrative of Sojourner Truth,* 21.

4. Truth and Gilbert, *Narrative of Sojourner Truth,* 21.

5. Tracey Michae'l Lewis-Giggetts, *Then They Came for Mine: Healing from the Trauma of Racial Violence* (Louisville, Ky.: Westminster John Knox, 2022), 89.

6. Hebrews 11:31, NKJV.

7. "Strong's G4102—Pistis," Blue Letter Bible, accessed August 28, 2023, www.blueletterbible.org/lexicon/g4102/nkjv/tr/0-1.

8. Becky Little, "How the US Got So Many Confederate Monuments," History.com, September 8, 2012, www.history.com/news/how-the-u-s-got-so-many-confederate-monuments.

9. Peter Holley and DeNeen L. Brown, "Woman Takes Down Confederate Flag in Front of South Carolina Statehouse," *The Washington Post,* June 27, 2015, www.washingtonpost.com/news/post-nation/wp/2015/06/27/woman-takes-down-confederate-flag-in-front-of-south-carolina-statehouse.

10. "2015: Charleston Church Shooting," History.com, June 8, 2020, www.history.com/this-day-in-history/charleston-ame-church-shooting.

11. Denise Lavoie and Alan Suderman, "Stonewall Jackson Removed from Richmond's Monument Avenue," Associated Press, July 1, 2020, https://apnews.com/article/us-news-ap-top-news-levar-stoney-richmond-virginia-b27b2bfce3ecefe13c917a69a59cd9da.

12. "Black Contractor Braves Threats in Removing Richmond Statues," NBC News, October 26, 2020, www.nbcnews.com/news/nbcblk/black-contractor-braves-threats-removing-richmond-statues-n1244772; Gregory S. Schneider, "White Contractors Wouldn't Remove Confederate Statues. So a Black Man Did It," *The Washington Post,* January 2, 2023, www.washingtonpost.com/dc-md-va/2023/01/02/devon-henry-confederate-statues-richmond.

13. Michael Schaub, "Texas Textbook Calling Slaves 'Immigrants' to Be Changed, After Mom's Complaint," *Los Angeles Times,* October 5, 2015, www.latimes.com/books/jacketcopy/la-et-jc-texas-textbook-calls-slaves-immigrants-20151005-story.html.

14. Brendan Koerner, "Where Did We Get Our Oath?," Slate, April 30, 2004, https://slate.com/news-and-politics/2004/04/how-the-courtroom-got-its-oath.html.

15. "PEN America Index of School Book Bans—Fall 2022," PEN America, accessed August 28, 2023, https://pen.org/index-of-school-book-bans-2022.

16. Kasey Meehan and Jonathan Friedman, "Banned in the USA: State Laws Supercharge Book Suppression in Schools," PEN America, April 20, 2023, https://pen.org/report/banned-in-the-usa-state-laws-supercharge-book-suppression-in-schools.

17. *Encyclopaedia Britannica,* s.v. "Ebony," last modified August 27, 2020, www.britannica.com/topic/Ebony-American-magazine; "Jet Magazine Returns with Cover Star Pinky Cole," TheGrio, April 11, 2023, https://thegrio.com/2023/04/11/the-return-of-jet-magazine.

18. N'dea Yancey-Bragg, "Florida School Receiving Death Threats After Turning Away 6-Year-Old with Dreadlocks," *USA Today,* August 16, 2018, www.usatoday.com/story/news/nation-now/2018/08/16/florida-school-faces-backlash-rejecting-6-year-old-dreadlocks/1010132002.

19. "Creating a Respectful and Open World for Natural Hair," The CROWN Act, accessed August 29, 2023, www.thecrownact.com/about.

20. Truth and Gilbert, *Narrative of Sojourner Truth,* 22.

21. Truth and Gilbert, *Narrative of Sojourner Truth,* 22.

22. Sojourner Truth, quoted in *The Anti-Slavery Bugle* (Salem, Ohio), June 21, 1851, https://chroniclingamerica.loc.gov/lccn/sn83035487/1851-06-21/ed-1/seq-4.

23. Darnella Frazier, Facebook video, May 26, 2020, www.facebook.com/darnellareallprettymarie/videos/1425398217661280.

24. Frazier, Facebook video, May 26, 2020.

25. Frazier, Facebook video, May 26, 2020.

26. Frazier, Facebook video, May 25, 2020.

27. Amos 5:24.

28. Hebrews 11:13, KJV.

## Chapter 10: The Black Love Lens: God's-Gifts

1. Michelle Singletary, "Black Americans Donate a Higher Share of Their Wealth Than Whites," *The Washington Post,* December 11, 2020, www.washingtonpost.com/business/2020/12/11/blacks-prioritize -philanthropy.

2. *Cultures of Giving: Energizing and Expanding Philanthropy by and for Communities of Color* (Battle Creek, Mich.: W. K. Kellogg Foundation, January 2012), 5, www.d5coalition.org/wp-content/uploads /2013/07/CultureofGiving.pdf.

3. Aditya Aladangady and Akila Forde, "Wealth Inequality and the Racial Wealth Gap," FEDS Notes, Board of Governors of the Federal Reserve System, October 22, 2021, https://doi.org/10.17016 /2380-7172.2861.

4. Singletary, "Black Americans Donate a Higher Share of Their Wealth Than Whites."

5. Luke 6:38.

6. Heralded as one of the most influential books by notable publications, including *The Chronicle of Higher Education,* Michelle Alexander's *The New Jim Crow: Mass Incarceration in the Age of Colorblindness* lays out how mass incarceration has robbed our Black Neighbors. Michelle Alexander, *The New Jim Crow: Mass Incarceration in the Age of Colorblindness* (New York: The New Press, 2012), 11.

7. John 2:1–10.

8. John 2:10.

9. Research has consistently shown that your Black Neighbors carry more educational debt than your other neighbors. For example, an article published by BestColleges showed that "Black adults carry the highest levels of student loan debt and are most likely to face repayment barriers." Lyss Welding, "Student Loan Debt by Race," BestColleges, June 16, 2023, www.bestcolleges.com/research/student -loan-debt-by-race.

## Chapter 11: The Black Love Lens: God's-Gifts from Partners-in-Love

1. Acts 4:32.

2. "Strong's G5485—Charis," Blue Letter Bible, accessed August 30, 2023, www.blueletterbible.org/lexicon/g5485/kjv/tr/0-1.

3. Acts 4:33.

4.   Acts 4:34–35.

5.   Acts 5:1–11.

6.   "Black Wall Street Neighbourhood, Tulsa, Oklahoma," Britannica: Geography & Travel, www.britannica.com/place/Black-Wall-Street.

7.   Nadia Joy Schult, " 'This Could Only Be God': Pastor Michael Todd Gives $1 Million to Tulsa Massacre Survivors, Black Nonprofits," Charisma News, June 28, 2021, www.charismanews.com/us/85901-this-could-only-be-god-pastor-michael-todd-gives-1-million-to-tulsa-massacre-survivors-black-nonprofits.

8.   Michael Todd, "Capital C Sunday // Change Starts in the Church // Devastation 2 Restoration," Transformation Church, June 20, 2021, video, 1:06:51, June 21, 2021, www.youtube.com/watch?v=Vt6_zZW_dew.

9.   Todd, "Capital C Sunday."

10.  2 Corinthians 9:7.

11.  Jeremiah 17:9.

12.  Romans 12:3.

13.  1 Chronicles 17:1.

14.  1 Chronicles 17:2.

15.  Isaiah 55:8–9.

16.  "Woman-Owned Businesses Are Growing 2X Faster on Average Than All Businesses Nationwide," American Express, September 23, 2019, www.americanexpress.com/content/amex/en-us/newsroom/articles/regions/woman-owned-businesses-are-growing-2x-faster-on-average-than.html.

17.  Donna Kelley, Mahdi Majbouri, and Angela Randolph, "Black Women Are More Likely to Start a Business Than White Men," *Harvard Business Review,* May 11, 2021, https://hbr.org/2021/05/black-women-are-more-likely-to-start-a-business-than-white-men; Susan Coleman, "The 'Liability of Newness' and Small Firm Access to Debt Capital: Is There a Link?," Pepperdine University, *The Journal of Entrepreneurial Finance 9,* no. 2 (Summer 2004): 39, https://digitalcommons.pepperdine.edu/cgi/viewcontent.cgi?article=1069&context=jef#:~:text=%E2%80%9CMature%E2%80%9D%20firms%20are%20firms%20older,and%20total%20number%20of%20employees.

18.  Liz Knueven, "The Barriers Black Families Face in Building

Generational Wealth," CNBC Select, May 26, 2023, www.cnbc.com /select/3-barriers-to-building-generational-wealth-for-black -families.

## Chapter 12: The Black Love Lens: The Spirit of Love

1. Acts 20:35.

2. Dr. Ken Fong, Facebook photo, August 31, 2022, www.facebook.com /photo?fbid=10160269421653769&set=pcb.10160269430368769.

3. Dr. Ken Fong, interview with author, January 20, 2023.

4. Rob Base and DJ E-Z Rock, "Joy and Pain," track 2 on *It Takes Two,* RCA Records, 1988.

5. Richard Bell, "Understanding the Fight Against Slavery," America's Long Struggle Against Slavery, The Great Courses, www.thegreat courses.com/courses/americas-long-struggle-against-slavery.

6. Jack Hayford, *Prayer Is Invading the Impossible* (Newberry, Fla.: Bridge-Logos, 1997), 64–65.

7. Ephesians 6:12, csb.

8. Galatians 6:9.

9. Madeleine L'Engle, *A Wrinkle in Time* (New York: Square Fish, 2007).

10. Psalm 18:34.

11. Charles Albert Tindley, "I'll Overcome Some Day," Hymnary.org, accessed September 1, 2023, https://hymnary.org/text/this_world _is_one_great_battlefield; Noah Adams, "The Inspiring Force of 'We Shall Overcome,'" NPR, August 28, 2013, www.npr.org /2013/08/28/216482943/the-inspiring-force-of-we-shall-overcome.

## Part Three: Go and Do Likewise

1. James Weldon Johnson, "Lift Every Voice and Sing," 1900, www .loc.gov/item/89751755.

## Chapter 13: Transforming the Road

1. John Wilkinson, "The Way from Jerusalem to Jericho," *Biblical Archaeologist* 38, no. 1 (1975): 10–24, www.jstor.org/stable/3209407.

2. Martin Luther King, Jr., "Beyond Vietnam—a Time to Break Silence" (sermon, Riverside Church, New York, N.Y., April 4, 1967), www.americanrhetoric.com/speeches/mlkatimetobreaksilence .htm.

3.  Mr. Humphreys's family of origin enslaved people on their property. It's likely that some of the money Mr. Humphreys gave was from the profits of the slave trade.

4.  "Exploring a National Treasure: Part 1," Cheyney University of Pennsylvania, accessed September 1, 2023, https://cheyney.edu/wp-content/uploads/2018/11/RichardHumphreys_QuakerPhilanthropist.pdf.

5.  Sojourner Ahébée, "'They See Me as a Role Model': Black Teachers Improve Education Outcomes for Black Students," WHYY, February 19, 2021, https://whyy.org/segments/they-see-me-as-a-role-model-black-teachers-improve-education-outcomes-for-black-students.

6.  There is a debate around if Cheyney or Lincoln University was the first HBCU. Cheyney was founded first but didn't provide baccalaureate degrees until 1914, after Lincoln had started to confer degrees. Janelle Harris Dixon, "Lincoln or Cheyney: Which Was the First HBCU?," The Root, April 29, 2014, www.theroot.com/lincoln-or-cheyney-which-was-the-first-hbcu-1790875485.

7.  "History of the Institute for Colored Youth," Villanova University, accessed September 1, 2023, https://exhibits.library.villanova.edu/index.php/institute-colored-youth/institute-history.

8.  "History of the Institute for Colored Youth," Villanova University.

9.  Jasmin Shupper, interview with author, July 17, 2023.

10.  Shupper, interview with author.

11.  Shupper, interview with author.

12.  Shupper, interview with author.

13.  Chanté Griffin, "How Natural Black Hair at Work Became a Civil Rights Issue," JSTOR Daily, July 3, 2019, https://daily.jstor.org/how-natural-black-hair-at-work-became-a-civil-rights-issue.

Chanté Griffin is a freelance journalist and natural hair advocate who writes extensively about race, culture, and faith. She's a contributing writer for *The Washington Post* and *Faithfully Magazine* and a former contributor to The Root and *L.A. Weekly.* Her articles, essays, and interviews have appeared in other publications including *HuffPost,* the *Los Angeles Times, The Christian Science Monitor, EBONY, Good Housekeeping, Literary Hub,* and Vogue.com.

Chanté has a deep love for God and a deep love for Black people. After college, she worked with Black collegians through a parachurch ministry; then she worked for an educational non-profit where she served Black and Latino/a K–12 students. Chanté was reared in the Church of God in Christ and today attends Vision Christian Fellowship, a non-denominational church in Pasadena, California. She's served at her church for the last decade, on the worship team, on the prayer team, and as an emcee.

Because Chanté believes the arts can ignite social change and soul transformation, she co-leads Spirit & Scribe, an online workshop that explores the intersection of writing craft and spiritual formation. In her free time, she enjoys praying, pretending she's a cast member on *Dancing with the Stars,* and making folks laugh via the @kinky _coily_comedy platform on Instagram.

To connect, visit @yougochante on Instagram, Twitter, or Facebook. To book for a speaking engagement, visit yougochante.com.

# ABOUT THE TYPE

This book was set in Granjon, a modern recutting of a typeface produced under the direction of George W. Jones (1860–1942), who based Granjon's design upon the letterforms of Claude Garamond (1480–1561). The name was given to the typeface as a tribute to the typographic designer Robert Granjon (1513–89).